No. 2872
$19.95

JET

82 CHALLENGING
NEW ADVENTURES

DAVE PROCHNOW

TAB BOOKS Inc.

Blue Ridge Summit, PA 17214

FIRST EDITION
FIRST PRINTING

Copyright © 1987 by TAB BOOKS Inc.
Printed in the United States of America

Reproduction or publication of the content in any manner, without express
permission of the publisher, is prohibited. No liability is assumed with respect to
the use of the information herein.

Library of Congress Cataloging in Publication Data

Prochnow, Dave.
JET: 82 challenging new adventures.

Includes index.
1. Flight simulators. 2. Airplanes—Piloting—
Data processing. I. Title
TL712.5.P75   1987   629.132′52′078   86-30012
ISBN 0-8306-0172-4
ISBN 0-8306-2872-X (pbk.)

Cover photograph courtesy of General Dynamics Corporation.

Contents

Part 2
JET Missions

Preface

Leading a small but profitable market of aero-software are three programs that represent over 90 percent of all flight simulator software sales. This trio—Flight Simulator, Flight Simulator II, and JET—are all designed by the same company—subLOGIC Corporation (whose name curiously sounds like a digital oxymoron). One plea that has been constantly voiced by owners of these programs concerns ideas for the creative use of this new-found computer flight ability. To a limited extent, subLOGIC has responded to this request by designing special scenery disks that allow the user to fly in different parts of the world. Unfortunately, scenery disks fail to satisfy the computer pilot's hunger for *action*. This book is the answer to this quest for action.

In its 12 chapters, this book captures all of the thrill and excitement of flight. For example, you'll be placed inside the cockpit of the world's first jet fighter and assigned to intercept Allied bomber formations over Europe. Later, you'll stress your jet flying skills to their limits with MiG/Phantom II combat in the skies of North Vietnam. Even high-performance aerobatics will be attempted in sections dealing with the Thunderbirds and Blue Angels professional aerial demonstration teams. No matter where a particular chapter takes you, however, the book's structure will have you successfully flying JET to complete your assigned mission.

Here are 82 different historical aviation scenarios for duplication with the subLOGIC JET software. Each of these scenarios follows a standard presentation format. By using this consistent format, each scenario can be quickly set up by the reader and "flown" on the computer without interrupting the action through constant text references. Furthermore, once the scenario has been completed, a mission debriefing will accurately judge the JET pilot's performance. This grading technique makes this book an interactive guide and not just another mundane sightseeing tour of JET scenery.

Concluding this book are three appendices that will enhance your overall enjoyment of the main text's aviation scenarios. One appendix offers the reader valuable reference material for dealing with the 82 scenarios. Appendix C is a complete visual identification guide to the aircraft that are presented in all 82 scenarios.

Appendices A and B are bonuses in a book of this nature. The first of these two appendices contains thumbnail reviews of the more popular flight simulation programs that can be found in today's market. Similarly, Appendix B supplies a complete program listing for your own flight simulator. Written in several of the more popular personal home computer BASIC dialects, this appendix will give you something else to fly when you're not engaged with one of the 82 JET scenarios.

As you duel Egyptian MiGs and strafe North Korean supply lines, remember that one over-riding factor separates you from the historical actions that you are simulating—survivability. In other words, if you get into trouble, you can always exit JET and restart the scenario. Where else can you climb into a multimillion-dollar jet fighter, dogfight hordes of enemy aircraft, crash your aircraft, and live to tell about it? Only JET—armed with this book—will ever give you this opportunity.

Acknowledgments

Two companies that provided extensive support during the preparation of this book are General Dynamics Corporation and subLOGIC Corporation. Their informational contributions helped fortify the factual accounts contained within this book.

Introduction:

Gear Down and Locked

Many critics argue that actual flight is difficult—if not impossible—to duplicate. They will state that although microcomputer-based flight simulation software makes a strong attempt at generating the "feel" of flying, there are several parameters that are still beyond even the most capable computer's abilities. These skeptics claim that the confinement of the cockpit, the sensation of movement, the feel of the engine's thrust, and the breathtaking beauty of aerial panoramic views serve as identifiable weaknesses in today's programming.

Balanced against these wholly negative views are the numerous merits of flight simulation programming. For example, fabulous graphics and stunning synthesized sound effects are quickly narrowing the distance between real flight and simulation with at least two of these previously listed shortcomings. Actually, these differences don't have to be completely eliminated; just lessening their disparity will help to validate computerized flight simulation as being realistic. Who knows, maybe someday you will "board" your computer and take an imaginary vacation flight, complete with passengers.

Oddly enough, flight simulators haven't always been the exclusive domain of microcomputers. Ed Link in 1929 sparked an interest in artificial flight with the development of his first primary Link Trainer. This early effort was crude by today's standards. Only a control yoke and rudder pedals served as controls for this early flight simulator. There was also a modest number of instruments to provide the pilot with a rudimentary indication of the craft's current flight orientation. The hallmark feature of the Link Trainer, however, was its ability to move proportionately in accordance with the movement of the yoke and rudder pedals. This movable trainer is in marked contrast with the current crop of stationary simulators. In fact, the Link Trainer's simulator movement did present several technical problems. Most of these problems centered around mechanical difficulties associated with the pneumatic bellows that provided the bulk of the Link Trainer's flight characteristics.

Eventually the Link Trainer caught the eye of a war-conscious Army Air Corps. Fueled by a desire to train pilots with a minimum of cost, the Army used an enhanced version of the Link Trainer for providing instructions to thousands of young cadets as a supplement to their Fairchild, Stearman, and Vultee flight training. The United States aerial achievements in the European and Pacific Theater of Operations during World War II indicate the success of this fledgling flight simulation program.

Even the movable Link Trainer suffered from similar losses in realism that have been previously identified as a peculiarity of the computer-based flight simulator. Therefore, the artificial production of aircraft movements does very little in enhancing the flight simulator's realistic qualities. This leaves only the confinement of the cockpit as the final barrier preventing the acceptance of flight simulation software. For the vast majority of simulator pilots, sitting in a straight-backed chair satisfies this requirement. If, on the other hand, you share the critics' viewpoint that the claustrophobic confines of a cockpit are vital to the success of a flight simulator, then operate your computer simulator while seated inside a closet.

Recognizing the realism limitations that are imposed on flight simulation software makes the achievement of subLOGIC Corporation even more outstanding. What started as a three-dimensional graphics demonstration program in 1979 by Bruce Artwick quickly mushroomed into the most popular flight simulator ever. Flight Simulator and Flight Simulator II place the computer user inside the cockpit of a piston-powered aircraft. From this vantage point, all of the controls, operations, and actions of this aircraft are realistically simulated.

Both Flight Simulator and Flight Simulator II dominated the computer airways for nearly seven years. In late 1985, several new flight simulation programs started to make significant inroads into the Flight Simulator market, however. Meeting this challenge, Artwick, Charles Guy, and subLOGIC released their first major new flight simulator in over six years. JET represented an enormous upgrade from the piston days of Flight Simulator. Now the computer user was thrust into the cockpit of either a General Dynamics F-16 Fighting Falcon (Fig. I-1) or a McDonnell Douglas F/A-18 Hornet. These high-performance jet aircraft stressed the very limits of current flight simulation technology.

Fig. I-1. The new General Dynamics F-16C Fighting Falcon. This aircraft is an improved variant of the F-16A. (courtesy General Dynamics Corp.)

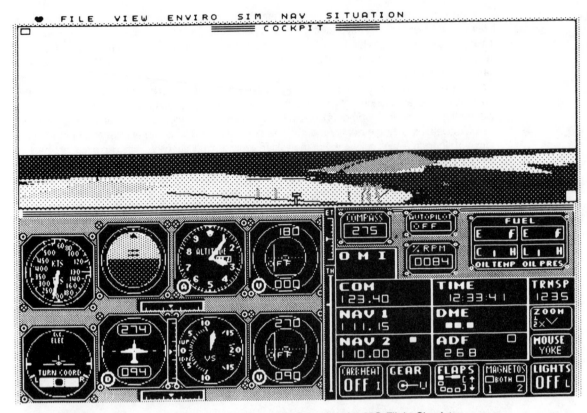

Fig. I-2. A forward view from the cockpit of the Macintosh Gates Learjet 25G Flight Simulator.

The single catch that restricted improvements in flight simulation software was identified by subLOGIC in 1986. Graphics imaging processing needed to be enhanced for both animation speed and image resolution. A graphics card for the IBM PC, the X-1 Graphics Board, was manufactured by subLOGIC as an alternative to increasing the graphics performance of the microcomputer. A special subLOGIC support software package, 3D Graphics, complemented the X-1 Graphics Board.

Interestingly enough, the 3D Graphics software contains the same drivers that generate the animation found on JET, Flight Simulator, and Flight Simulator II. Theoretically, the next generation of flight simulation programs could come from this powerful hardware/software animation combination. The realization of this point would be indeed ironic, as subLOGIC would still be directing the path of flight simulators, but from an entirely different perspective.

Continuing the quest for realistic flight simulation software even further, subLOGIC is currently updating a thorough set of scenery disks. This scenery software is for use in conjunction with Flight Simulator, Flight Simulator II, and JET. Basically, these disks contain massive graphics databases that provide detailed ground imagery for selected areas around the world. Cities, buildings, highways, and other noteworthy landmarks are all painstakingly digitized on these scenery disks. By using these special scenery disks, the Flight Simulator II pilot can land at a detailed airport in Osaka, Japan, or JET can be flown on a high-performance mission over San Francisco Bay.

In addition to providing the scenery disks, subLOGIC is constantly translating all three of its flight simulation programs into versions that will operate on the most popular microcomputers.

This translation process includes making Flight Simulator available for the Apple Computer Macintosh (Fig. I-2), the Atari 520ST and 1040ST, and the Commodore Amiga. One problem that was initially encountered with these particular translations was in adapting the user interface from a keyboard/joystick combination to a keyboard/mouse operation (Fig. I-3). The success of this modification is best judged by taking one of these 68000-based versions of Flight Simulator up for a test flight. Following this evaluation, even the staunchest joystick jockey will find that total control is not only possible but extremely realistic through the clicking and dragging movements of the mouse.

There are two different aircraft available in JET: a General Dynamics F-16 Fighting Falcon and a McDonnell Douglas F/A-18 Hornet. The performance characteristics of these two aircraft make it easy for either one of them to "outfly" the simulator pilot. For this reason, an extensive training program is presented in Part I of this book. Read and understand the four chapters in this portion of the book before attempting any of the historical aviation scenarios that are discussed in Part II. Remember, only through careful training can a jet mission be successfully completed.

Including the F-16 and the F/A-18 in JET provides the computer user with the unique opportunity to pilot two of the United States' top-of-the-line fighter/attack aircraft. Gone are the days of 150 knot airspeeds and limited aerobatic capability. These jets can climb to altitudes in excess of 50,000 feet at supersonic speeds. In fact, once you have completed your advanced jet fighter training in Part I, you will be able to take off either the F-16 or the F/A-18, assume a 90-degree vertical climb, and accelerate to an altitude of 30,000 feet in under 40 seconds.

These fighter types that are used in JET offer a smorgasbord of high-performance specifications. Starting with the land-based F-16, the simulator pilot will be flying an aircraft with a 30 foot wingspan and a 49 foot 10.5 inch total length. The maximum takeoff weight for the F-16A variant is 27,000 pounds. Power for this aircraft comes from a single Pratt & Whitney F100-PW-100 turbofan engine that is capable of 23,500 pounds of thrust. In flight, the F-16A can reach a maximum speed of 1,466 mph and an altitude in excess of 60,000 feet. Armaments are varied according to the F-16's mission. This same approach is duplicated in JET.

Following in a similar mold, the carrier-based F/A-18 measures 40 feet 4.8 inches across its wings and 56 feet from nose probe to tail. A maximum combat takeoff weight of 51,900 pounds is made possible through two General Electric F404-GE-400 turbofan engines generating 16,000 pounds of thrust each. A maximum speed of 1,190 mph and altitudes above 60,000 feet are possible with the F/A-18A variant. Underwing and fuselage weapon stores are the real virtue of the F/A-18. Like the F-16, however, these armaments are modified to reflect the current mission.

Two interesting technological developments help make flying the F-16 and F/A-18 less demanding on the pilot. The first is the "fly-by-wire" control surface actuator system. Instead of having the usual mechanical assortment of rods, cables, and linkages that are used for moving the control surfaces, these fly-by-wire fighters use a network of electrically controlled servoactuators for maintaining control surface movement. There are numerous advantages to this method of control. The most important of these benefits is a reduction in weight. Additionally, more precise and responsive control is possible with the servoactuators. Finally, less room is consumed by the electrical wiring than with a comparable mechanical system. This results in increased fuel storage capacity. An interesting sidelight to the fly-by-wire system is its unusual method of system redundancy. In this case, all mechanical backup systems have been eliminated. Alternatively, fly-by-wire aircraft use multiple signal channels for sending the valuable control data to the servoactuators. Therefore, if one of the channels is disrupted, there is another channel for operating the control surface. Of course, a substantial dose of EMP (electromagnetic pulse) will shoot the whole system.

The second luxury found on both the F-16 and the F/A-18 is the head-up display (HUD). This is a transparent screen that is located directly in line with the pilot's forward vision. All of the aircraft's vital information is contained on the HUD through a special projection technique

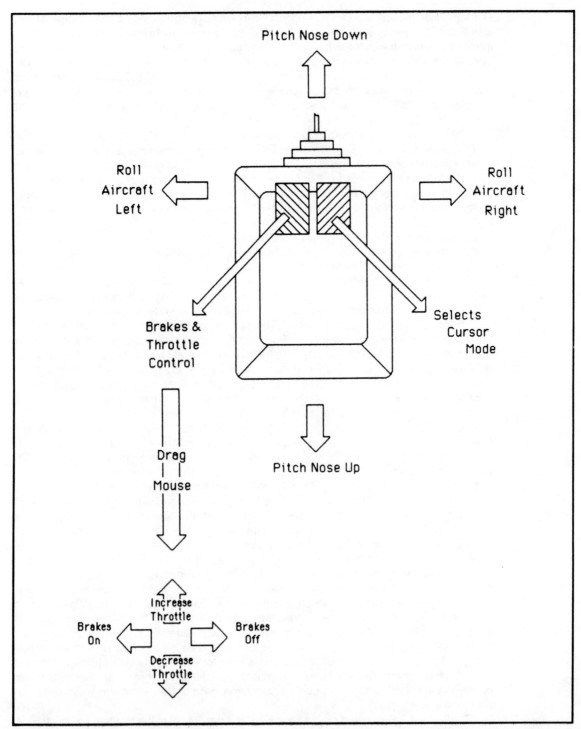

Fig. I-3. The diversity in function assigned to the Amiga mouse makes this odd user interface an ideal complement to the flight simulator.

that makes the data appear to "float" on the screen. Using a grease pencil to write pertinent travel information on your automobile's windshield while driving would produce a comparable effect—although with the HUD, all of the superimposed information is constantly updated during the course of the aircraft's mission. Therefore, the pilot can receive a continuous reading of the aircraft's flight characteristics and current weapons status without looking away from the cockpit's forward view.

Remarkably, both of these advanced fighter features are found in JET. You will find that the control surfaces offer the same precise and delicate "feel" as those found on the full-size F-16 and F/A-18. Additionally, every command maneuver will begin immediately upon execution. The end result is that all of the sluggishness found in piston-engined flight simulation software has been eliminated from this jet-age simulator. Unfortunately, a potentially bad side effect from the fly-by-wire control system is that the beginning pilot will have a tendency to overfly the aircraft. In other words, too much movement will be signaled to the control surface and a gross maneuver will be the result. Attempting to compensate for this error, the pilot will then overcorrect the initial maneuver and compound the mistake with an exaggerated movement in the opposite direction. All is not lost, however. The fly-by-wire system can be mastered after several simulated hours of logged flight time.

Even the HUD can be potentially disorienting on the pilot's initial JET encounter. Once again, flying several simulated missions will familiarize the jet pilot with the use of the HUD. Then, after you thoroughly understand the operation of the HUD, you will be able to customize its displayed information for your particular mission. This piloting technique does require a complete mastery of the keyboard (and joystick, if you elect to use this optional element) and its associated control locations. The four chapters in Part 1 will provide you with all of the instruction necessary for learning the computer interface, manipulating the HUD, and operating the control surfaces. Even if you are a veteran jet jock, you should complete the solo test that is found in Chapter 4 and earn your wings prior to attempting any of the 82 historical aviation scenarios that are depicted in Part 2.

Part 1
JET Flight Training

Chapter 1

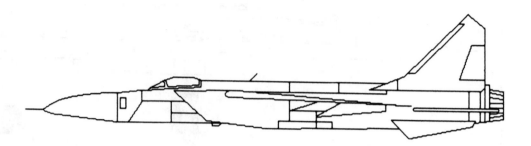

Aircraft and Computer Flight

The essence of flight is air movement. Governing the movement of this air are specific physical laws. These laws and their associated principles are the invisible forces that make an aircraft fly. Whether the air is moving around your automobile driving along the highway or speeding past the nose of a supersonic jet aircraft, the application of these laws remains the same. Adhere to these laws and the object will possess aerodynamic properties. Conversely, violate these basic physical principles and the flow of air will be disrupted and flight will be negated.

AERODYNAMICS

There are four forces that act on the aerodynamics of an object: lift, gravity, thrust, and drag. Figure 1-1 demonstrates the action that these four forces exert on an aircraft in flight. By successfully juggling these four forces, *any* object can be made to fly. (A whimsical extension of this statement is voiced by McDonnell-Douglas F-4 Phantom II pilots, who claim that the F-4 proved the point that given enough thrust, even a brick can fly.)

Lift. *Lift*, the first of these forces, serves as the major reason that an aircraft flies. Air moving across the upper and lower surfaces of a wing produces the necessary lift for flight. When dealing with flight, lift must be strong enough to counteract the force of gravity. Therefore, in order to generate the required degree of lift, special aerodynamic features must be applied to the wing. The leading feature in making the needed lift is the *airfoil* of the wing.

Airfoils serve two functions in generating lift on a wing: reducing turbulence and increasing the wing's upper surface distance. The reduction in turbulence is necessary for minimizing the amount of flight-destroying *drag* (Fig. 1-2), whereas the increased upper surface distance results in a lower atmospheric pressure for air moving over the wing. While the concept of reduced turbulence is relatively easy to grasp, the notion of a greater distance producing a lowered air pressure deserves some further elaboration.

In the mid-1700s a Swiss mathematician named Daniel Bernoulli postulated that the pressure of a gas decreases as the speed of the gas increases. Today, over 200 years after its discovery, Bernoulli's principle still dictates the design of airfoils. By studying the shape of a basic

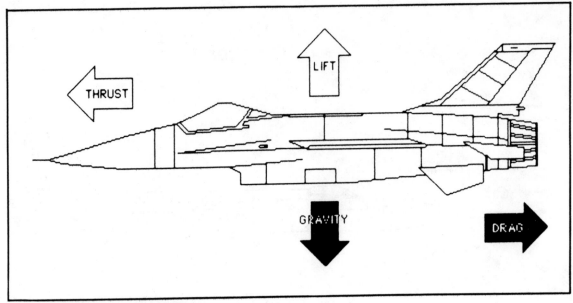

Fig. 1-1. The four forces that affect flight.

airfoil (Fig. 1-3), the full impact on lift that is made by this gas law can be visualized.

The upper surface of a wing is generally curved. This curved airfoil shape makes the distance over the wing's upper surface, from the leading edge to its trailing edge, longer than the same distance over the wing's flatter bottom surface. Due to this increased distance, air moving around this airfoil will move faster across the upper surface than across the bottom surface. Therefore, this faster-moving air will create a lower air pressure over the wing's upper surface. The final result from this increased pressure underneath the wing is lift.

Several other factors can affect the total lift produced by the airfoil of a wing. Increasing the wing's angle into the moving air increases the speed of the air moving over the upper surface. In turn, this creates greater lift. The angle formed by the wing and the moving air is called the *angle of attack*. Lift is destroyed when the angle of attack is increased to a point where turbulence is produced on the wing's upper surface. This effect is known as a *stall*. A stall can be counteracted by another lift-producing agent—airspeed. Increased airspeed also raises the pres-

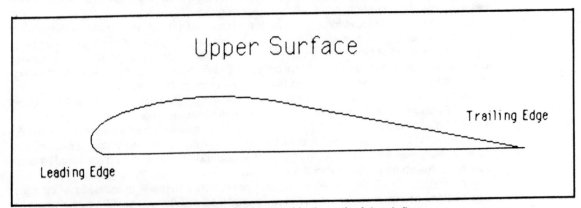

Fig. 1-2. A stylized airfoil, where the leading edge is placed in the path of the air flow.

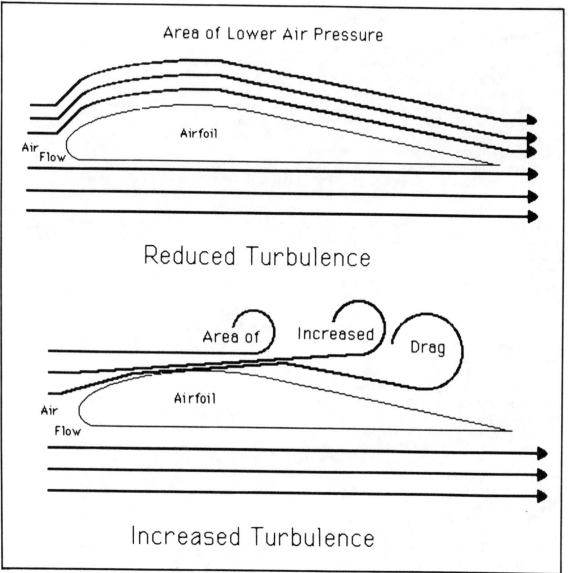

Area of Lower Air Pressure

Airfoil

Air Flow

Reduced Turbulence

Area of Increased Drag

Airfoil

Air Flow

Increased Turbulence

Fig. 1-3. Under normal flight conditions, air moves smoothly over the upper surface of an airfoil. If this flow is disrupted, however, increased turbulence will cause drag and reduce the airfoil's lift.

sure difference between the wing's upper and lower surfaces, which results in greater lift. As a rule, the square of the airspeed equals the amount of increase in lift.

One last item concerning lift deals with two control surfaces that can be attached to a wing for increased lift. A *slot* is a movable opening that is usually located along the leading edge of a wing. Using a slot delays the point at which a wing will stall. Therefore, when a slot is extended, the pilot is able to fly at a slower speed and still retain increased lift.

The other control surface is the *flap*. Flaps are downward-moving sections found along a wing's trailing edge. Lowering a flap exaggerates the curvature of the wing's airfoil. The enlarged size of the airfoil slows the speed of the aircraft as well as increasing the wing's lift. Flaps are best used during landings. There are times, however, when the increased lift (in spite of the decreased airspeed) is desired during takeoffs.

Gravity. The negative force that fights the lift of a wing is the weight of the aircraft, or the gravitational pull of the earth. Basically, the aircraft must overcome the effects of gravity in order to fly. Once an aircraft achieves level flight, however, the combination of gravity and lift must equal zero. Otherwise, the aircraft would either drop, when gravity is greater than lift, or continually climb, if lift were greater than gravity.

Another important aspect of gravity is that the aircraft must possess a point where the entire weight of the plane is equally displaced. This balance point or the *center of gravity* for the aircraft must rest within the wing's *center of lift*. Successfully mating these two points determines the final stability and flight characteristics of the aircraft.

Generally speaking, the wing's center of lift is at a point that is one-fourth of the distance from the leading edge to the trailing edge. Bringing the center of gravity ahead of this point will result in an aircraft that is nose-heavy. Likewise, placing the center of gravity behind this point produces a tail-heavy aircraft.

Once the center of gravity has been correctly placed on the center of lift, the aircraft's three axes of movement can be established (Fig. 1-4). These three axes form the basis for the control of an aircraft's flight. Moving the aircraft's nose up and down rotates around the *pitch* axis. Movement around the *yaw* axis causes the aircraft's nose to travel horizontally from side to side. The last axis, the *roll* axis, represents the movement from the aircraft's wingtips being alternately raised and lowered.

There are several control surfaces located on the wing and on the tail that move the aircraft around these three axes. The *elevator* handles the pitch axis. Yaw is controlled by the *rudder*. Lastly, a pair of *ailerons* control an aircraft's roll. The full effect of these three control surfaces will be more fully explained in the next section.

Only through the precise movement of these three control surfaces can an aircraft be correctly flown. Failure to master coordination between the three control surfaces can result in some unwanted flight characteristics. For example, the exclusive use of the rudder in a bank or turn produces excessive yaw. This overabundance of yaw will cause the tail of the aircraft to skid away from the turn. Similarly, relying on ailerons exclusively in a bank or turn generates too much roll. The increased roll makes the aircraft slip into the turn. One final control failure can turn into disaster. While a stall in itself can be a life-threatening loss of pitch control, the liberal application of rudder during a stall overloads the yaw axis and produces a spin. The end result from a spin is often the loss of the aircraft. Unfortunately, the disoriented pilot will usually meet the same fate as the aircraft.

Thrust. Pushing the aircraft forward is the force of *thrust*. The thrust necessary for moving the aircraft can be produced by a number of different means. Piston engines driving propellers and turbojet turbines providing jet propulsion are the two most common methods of generating thrust. In the case of the propeller, thrust is developed by the shape of the individual propeller blades. Each blade has an airfoil shape. This airfoil, like its counterpart found in a wing, creates a region of low pressure on its upper surface and a region of higher pressure along the bottom surface. Therefore, with the propeller blade's upper surface facing away from the aircraft, the difference in air pressure on each blade forces the aircraft to move forward.

An interesting extension of the standard propeller is the *variable-pitch* propeller. This propeller is able to produce greater thrust by altering the blades' angle of attack. In order to change the propeller's pitch, the pilot merely rotates a pitch dial inside the cockpit. Additionally, there is an extreme setting on the pitch control that places each blade parallel to the aircraft's fuselage. This condition is known as a *feathered* propeller. Feathering is usually applied to a faulty engine as a precaution against catastrophic disaster.

Countering the force of thrust is *drag*. During takeoff, thrust must be greater than drag. Once level flight is reached, however, both thrust and drag are equal. If thrust were unbridled from

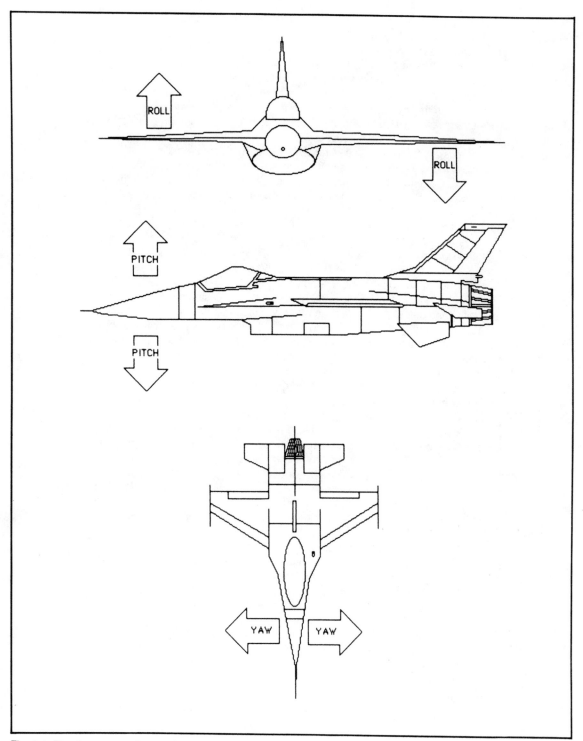

Fig. 1-4. The three axes of controlled aircraft movement.

the negating effects of drag, the aircraft would constantly accelerate. This cancellation prevents the problems associated with continuous acceleration.

Switching from propeller thrust to jet thrust does increase the speed of the aircraft. Thrust from a jet engine differs from that produced by a propeller. With a jet engine, a reaction is produced inside the engine through the burning of fuel and the compression of air. The force of this reaction is directed out the rear of the jet engine. As this controlled combustion is expelled, the engine "reacts" by moving in the opposite direction from the exhaust.

Jet engine power is measured in *pounds of thrust*. In comparing jet thrust to propeller thrust, one horsepower is equal to one pound of thrust at 375 mph. Therefore, at lower speeds jets offer few thrust advantages over propeller-driven aircraft. This equality differs dramatically at higher speeds. A jet engine delivering 10,000 pounds of thrust at 750 mph is equal to a 20,000 horsepower engine. Similarly, in jet engines, as thrust and airspeed increase, the total engine horsepower also increases. Conversely, physical limitations in the operation of a propeller prevent such significant horsepower production.

One important attribute of the enormous power capabilities of the jet engine is found in flying at great speeds. These great aircraft speeds can reach a point exceeding the speed of sound. Supersonic speeds are usually expressed by a *Mach number*. Basically, Mach 1 equals the speed of sound at a given altitude. For example, sound travels at 760 mph at sea level. Therefore, an aircraft traveling at 760 mph would be moving at Mach 1 at this altitude. By increasing altitude, however, it is also possible to increase the Mach number without increasing the airspeed (due to sound's decreased speed at higher altitudes). In other words, an aircraft going 760 mph at 40,000 feet has a Mach number of 1.15. Comparing these two examples, it is easy to see how the exclusive use of the Mach number can cause confusion (e.g., 874 mph at sea level equals Mach 1.15). Combining a reference altitude with each Mach value eliminates this arbitrariness.

Drag. Negating the effects of thrust is the force of *drag*. Every air disturbance generated by the aircraft produces drag. This disturbance can be caused by the fuselage, canopy, and even rivets in the skin of the aircraft. Special streamlining techniques are used to minimize the production of drag. Even an aerodynamically clean aircraft still creates drag.

Skin friction is the leading cause of drag. Basically, the layer of air next to the aircraft's skin rubs against the air moving by the aircraft, which results in friction. There are two flow patterns exhibited by the movement of air between these two layers: *laminar flow* and *turbulent flow*. Laminar flow is a smooth flow of air that is generally found on the forward portion of an aircraft. An aircraft surrounded by laminar flow would have very little drag. As the air moves along the surfaces of the aircraft, however, it increases in both turbulence and friction. This movement of air is called turbulent flow. Minimizing the formation of turbulent airflow is the best method for reducing skin friction and drag.

A technique known as *boundary-layer control* helps in preventing the development of turbulent airflow. Special porous aircraft skins, along with high-pressure vacuum pumps, help to smooth out turbulent airflow patterns. Forestalling the occurrence of turbulent flow keeps an aircraft's drag to a minimum. A fringe benefit of boundary-layer control when applied to the upper surface of an aircraft's wing is that it can also reduce the wing's ability to stall. This reduced stall capability gives an aircraft greater low-speed handling and increased takeoff and landing performance.

When dealing with jet aircraft an additional form of drag is possible. Flying at supersonic speeds violently disturbs the surrounding air, causing a shock wave. This shock wave raises the drag of the aircraft. The increased drag of supersonic flight is offset by higher jet engine thrust and the employment of area-rule principles in design. The *area-rule principle* is a special supersonic aircraft feature in which the fuselage becomes narrower at the wing attachment point (Fig. 1-5). This slight indentation of the fuselage results in a reduction in drag and, correspondingly, an increase in speed.

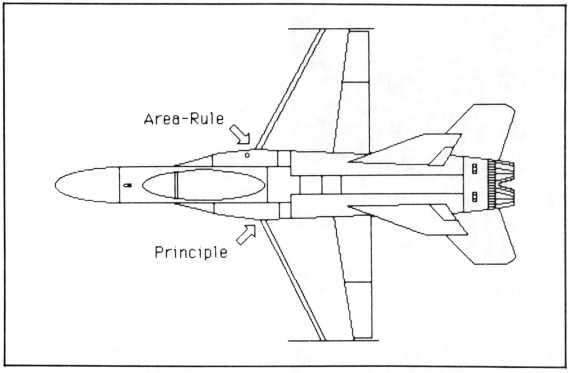

Area-Rule

Principle

Fig. 1-5. The F/A-18 is an ideal representative of the area rule principle. This narrowing at the fuselage/wing juncture reduces the drag caused by supersonic flight.

AIRCRAFT CONTROLS

Controlling an aircraft in flight involves a dazzling array of instruments and a large assortment of control devices. All of this instrumentation fills an area of the aircraft called the *cockpit* (Figs. 1-6, 1-7). The central control found in the cockpit is the control *yoke*. Various names have been applied to the control yoke, including *joystick,* wheel, and controller. No matter which name it uses, the control yoke serves as a direct physical connection between the pilot and the ailerons and the elevators. Additionally, two foot pedals give the pilot control over the movement of the aircraft's rudder. Therefore, all three axes of movement can be manipulated by the pilot by using the control yoke and the rudder pedals.

Pulling the control yoke back or pushing it forward moves the elevators up and down, respectively. The movement of the elevators, in turn, causes the aircraft to pitch up and down, respectively (Fig. 1-8). The final effect of this movement is that the aircraft will either climb or dive.

Moving the control yoke from side to side alternately raises the aileron of one wing while lowering the aileron of the other wing. This movement rolls the aircraft in the direction of the raised aileron (Fig. 1-9). In other words, when the control yoke is moved to the left, the left wing aileron is raised and the right wing aileron is lowered. Similarly, when the control yoke is moved to the right, the left wing aileron is lowered and the right wing aileron is raised. The effect of this aileron movement is that in the first case the aircraft will roll to the left and in the second example the aircraft rolls to the right.

In today's modern jet aircraft, many functions have been affixed to the control yoke. The control yoke's high command density is dictated by the need for a lightning-quick reaction time

9

Fig. 1-6. Entry into the cockpit is usually gained through a movable canopy. In this F-4E, the pilot and the WSO sit in two separate, tandem cockpits.

in a supersonic aircraft. For example, on the McDonnell Douglas F/A-18, in addition to the control yoke's standard elevator/aileron control, the Hornet pilot is also able to operate:

- ☐ sensor control (four positions)
- ☐ air-to-ground weapon release
- ☐ gun/missiles trigger
- ☐ nosewheel steering
- ☐ auto pilot disengage
- ☐ pitch and roll trim
- ☐ air-to-air weapon select (three positions)

Based on this diversity in function, it is easy to see why the control yoke is called the controller in modern jet fighters.

The final control device is the pair of rudder pedals that are located on the cockpit's floor. Only one rudder pedal is pushed at a time with the pilot's foot. This pushing causes the aircraft to rotate about the yaw axis (Fig. 1-10). As an example, when the pilot pushes the left rudder pedal, the rudder moves to the left. This makes the aircraft's nose yaw to the left. Likewise, when the pilot pushes the right rudder pedal, the rudder moves to the right. This rightward rudder movement causes the aircraft's nose to yaw to the right. Interestingly enough, the rudder pedals serve

Fig. 1-7. Many sophisticated design improvements are found in the F-16A's cockpit. The HUD instrumentation is projected onto the square glass panel located in the pilot's forward field of view. The control yoke or controller is located on the right side of the pilot's seat. (courtesy General Dynamics Corp.)

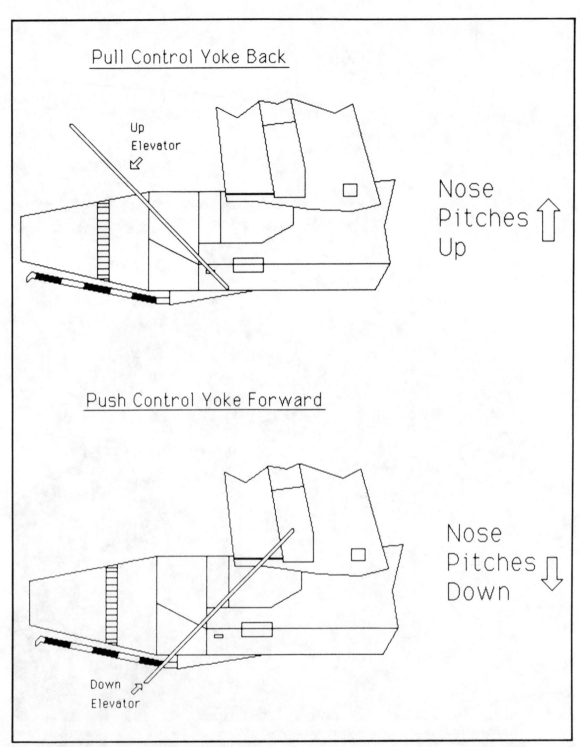

Fig. 1-8. Elevator movement controls the pitch of the aircraft.

Move Control Yoke Left

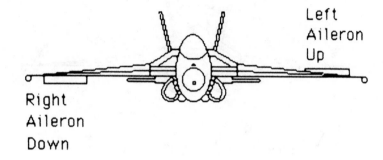

Left
Aileron
Up

Right
Aileron
Down

Rolls Aircraft Left

Move Control Yoke Right

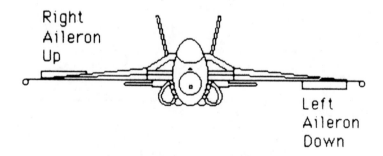

Right
Aileron
Up

Left
Aileron
Down

Rolls Aircraft Right

Fig. 1-9. Aileron movement controls the roll of the aircraft.

Push Left Rudder Pedal

Left Rudder

Yaws Nose Left

Push Right Rudder Pedal

Right Rudder

Yaws Nose Right

Fig. 1-10. Rudder movement controls the yaw of the aircraft.

two different functions when the aircraft is on the ground.

Once an aircraft is on the ground, the vast majority of its airspeed has been eliminated. This loss in air movement reduces the effectiveness of the aircraft's control surfaces for directing the movement of the aircraft. In order to compensate for this loss of function, the rudder pedals take on a new role when the aircraft taxis about the ground. The rudder pedals are now used for moving either the nose or tailwheel (the exact wheel location is dependent on the landing gear configuration). By using the rudder pedals in this fashion, an aircraft's ground movement becomes just a matter of steering.

Another ground function of the rudder pedals is the operation of the brakes. These brakes are located in the main wheels of the landing gear. By pushing both of the rudder pedals simultaneously, the wheel brakes are engaged and any rolling movement of the aircraft is stopped. Don't confuse the function of these wheel brakes with either the operation or the action of the *air brake* or *speed brake*. The speed brake is only deployed during flight and drastically reduces an aircraft's airspeed.

During flight, maintaining a true level aircraft attitude can require that the pilot hold continual adjustments on the control surfaces. In the course of a prolonged mission, the constant application of this force can fatigue the pilot. Therefore, small auxiliary control surfaces are found on the elevators, ailerons, and rudder. These smaller surfaces are called *trim tabs*. Trim tabs share the same control principles as the larger control surfaces. By setting these trim tabs, the flight of the aircraft can be balanced, thereby freeing the pilot from having to exert a constant pressure on the control surfaces. Trimming an aircraft is not the same as using a flight computer or autopilot function. Trim tabs merely aid in the balancing of an aircraft's control surfaces while in level flight.

Using just the rudder or just the ailerons for turning an aircraft will result in some undesirable side effects. Skids and slips disrupt attempts at rudder-only and aileron-only banks. Therefore, coordinated control surface applications are used during all formal turns and banks. A coordinated turn or bank combines both rudder and aileron movement. In a right bank, for example, both right rudder and right aileron are applied at the same time (a touch of up elevator might also be necessary). The resulting turn will be smooth and devoid of any skids or slips. This is called a *coordinated turn*. There are times, however, when coordinated control movement is unwanted. Aerobatics is a good example where uncoordinated movements are requisite. JET flies with only coordinated banks. Unfortunately, this coordinated movement can't be overridden for aerobatic purposes. In spite of this limitation, Chapter 3 provides several tricks for making JET fully aerobatic.

COMPUTER CONTROLS

JET uses 42 to 46 different control commands (depending on the type of computer). All of these commands are operated through keyboard keystrokes. Alternatively, an optional joystick can be used for the manipulation of the aircraft's control surfaces. Table 1-1 lists all of the JET commands for the Apple II family of computers. The Commodore 64/128 computer's commands, on the other hand, are listed in Table 1-2. With the exception of three controls, the commands listed in this table also correspond to those used on the IBM PCjr. The target selection, menu, and screen centering controls on the IBM PCjr follow the keyboard structure of the IBM PC version. These IBM PC commands are listed in Table 1-3. The terminology that is used for identifying each JET control in these tables will be used throughout the remainder of this book. This universal language makes the instruction that is presented in the later chapters much clearer and easier to understand. For example, the command "engage the speed brake" is interpreted as meaning:

Press the Shift + B key combination for the Commodore 64/128.
Press the Shift + B key combination for the IBM PCjr.
Press the B key for the IBM PC.

As an instructional aid, you may wish to make a copy of the required table and place it next to your keyboard during JET flight.

HARDWARE SYSTEM REQUIREMENTS

The actual computer hardware that is required for flying JET varies according to each particular computer brand. Along with these different hardware requirements are equally different sets of startup instructions.

Table 1-1. JET Keyboard Commands for Apple II Computers.

Command	Keystroke
Afterburner Disengage	Left Arrow
Afterburner Engage	Full Throttle & Press Right Arrow
Attitude Indicator Off	A
Attitude Indicator On	A
Backward View	5 + B
Bank Left	F
Bank Right	H
Control Tower Viewpoint Mode	C
Drop Bomb	Space
Eject	Control + E
Exit *JET*	Esc
Fire Gun	Space
Fire Missile	Space
Forward View	5 + T
Joystick Enable/Center	Control + J
Joystick Disable	Control + J
Landing Gear Extend	Control + G
Landing Gear Retract	Control + G
Left View	5 + F
Neutralize Bank	G
Neutralize Pitch	G
Neutralize Roll	G
Pause with Message	P
Pause without Message	Control + P
Pilot Viewpoint Mode	C
Pitch Nose Down	T
Pitch Nose Up	B
Radar System Display Off	W
Radar System Display On	W
Right View	5 + H
Roll Left	F-Hold
Roll Right	H-Hold
Scenary Data Base Reload	Control + S
Select Target	;
Sound Off	S
Sound On	S
Speedbrake Disengage	Control + B
Speedbrake Engage	Control + B
Throttle Decrease	Left Arrow
Throttle Increase	Right Arrow
Upward View	5 + G
View Magnification Decrease	N
View Magnification Increase	Y
Weapon System Select	Return
Weapon Tracking System Off	R
Weapon Tracking System On	R

Table 1-2. JET Keyboard Commands for the Commodore 64 and Commodore 128 Computers.

Command	Keystroke
Afterburner Disengage	-
Afterburner Engage	Full Throttle & Press +
Attitude Indicator Off	A
Attitude Indicator On	A
Backward View	5 + B
Bank Left	F
Bank Right	H
Control Tower Viewpoint Mode	C
Drop Bomb	Space
Eject	Shift + E
Exit *JET*	Run/Stop
Fire Gun	Space
Fire Missile	Space
Forward View	5 + T
Landing Gear Extend	Shift + G
Landing Gear Retract	Shift + G
Left View	5 + F
Neutralize Bank	G
Neutralize Pitch	G
Neutralize Roll	G
Pause	P
Pilot Viewpoint Mode	C
Pitch Nose Down	T
Pitch Nose Up	B
Radar System Display Off	W
Radar System Display On	W
Right View	5 + H
Roll Left	F-Hold
Roll Right	H-Hold
Select Target	Up Arrow
Sound Off	S
Sound On	S
Speedbrake Disengage	Shift + B
Speedbrake Engage	Shift + B
Throttle Decrease	-
Throttle Increase	+
Upward View	5 + G
View Magnification Decrease	N
View Magnification Increase	Y
Weapon System Select	Return
Weapon Tracking System Off	R
Weapon Tracking System On	R

Table 1-3. JET Keyboard Commands for IBM PC Computers.

Command	Keystroke
Afterburner Disengage	-
Afterburner Engage	Full Throttle & Press +
Attitude Indicator Off	A
Attitude Indicator On	A
Backward View	Scroll Lock + Cursor Down
Bank Left	Cursor Left
Bank Right	Cursor Right
Center the Screen	Tab
Control Tower Viewpoint Mode	C
Drop Bomb	Space
Eject	Shift + E
Exit *JET*	Escape
Fire Gun	Space
Fire Missile	Space
Forward View	Scroll Lock + Cursor Up
Landing Gear Extend	G
Landing Gear Retract	G
Left View	Scroll Lock + Cursor Left
Neutralize Bank	Numeric Keypad 5
Neutralize Pitch	Numeric Keypad 5
Neutralize Roll	Numeric Keypad 5
Pause	P
Pilot Viewpoint Mode	C
Pitch Nose Down	Cursor Up
Pitch Nose Up	Cursor Down
Radar System Display Off	W
Radar System Display On	W
Right View	Scroll Lock + Cursor Right
Roll Left	Cursor Left-Hold
Roll Right	Cursor Right-Hold
Select Target	Backspace
Sound Off	S
Sound On	S
Speedbrake Disengage	B
Speedbrake Engage	B
Throttle Decrease	-
Throttle Increase	+
Upward View	Scroll Lock + Numeric Keypad 5
View Magnification Decrease	Page Down
View Magnification Increase	Page Up
Weapon System Select	Return
Weapon Tracking System Off	R
Weapon Tracking System On	R

Apple. Virtually any "standard" Apple II computer is able to run JET. This all-inclusive blanket statement represents the following Apple computer models: Apple II, Apple II+, Apple IIe, and Apple IIc. Apple compatible computers (such as the Franklins, Laser 128, and Apple IIGS) should also run JET, although the veracity of this speculation has not been proven.

Besides the Apple II computer, you will also need a floppy disk drive and a monitor for flying JET. An optional joystick can be added to this arrangement for controlling the aircraft's three axes of movement and firing the selected weapon system.

The joystick that can be added to the flight system is of questionable value, however. Due to the large number of keyboard-based instrument controls, joystick flight can be impractical. Moving your hands back and forth between the keyboard and the joystick frustrates the smooth operation of the jet aircraft. In light of all of these negative aspects, a joystick does lend an air of realism to the flight simulator. Therefore, if you demand this level of realistic flight, plug the joystick into the Apple's joystick port.

After you have assembled all of the required hardware, it is time to start the program. Only two steps are necessary for beginning JET:

1. Place the JET floppy disk in disk drive 1 of your Apple computer system.
2. Turn on the computer. (This method is the auto-boot starting technique.)

2a. Alternatively, if your computer is already on, insert the JET disk into disk drive 1 and press the Control + Open Apple + Reset key combination.

When the program has been loaded, you are presented with a menu for selecting the type of monitor that you are using.

An Apple system with a color monitor:
Press A.
An Apple system with a monochrome monitor:
Press B.
Your Apple system is now ready for jet flight.

Commodore. Commodore 64/128 computer owners will need very little "extra" equipment in order to fly JET. In addition to the C-64 or C-128, only a floppy disk drive and a monitor are necessary for completing your jet fighter flight simulator. You may also add an optional joystick for moving the aircraft's three axes' control surfaces.

Setting up your flight simulator is remarkably easy. The floppy disk drive can be either the older single-sided Commodore 1541 or the newer double-sided Commodore 1571. Whichever model is used, connect it to the computer's serial plug.

Next, attach your monitor to the computer's rf (Radio Frequency) output socket. If you are using a television set (either color or black and white) as your monitor, then you might need to attach a TV switch box between the Commodore's rf plug and the TV's antenna leads. Some of the more recent models of television sets incorporate a special game plug into their design, thereby eliminating the need for this box. If, on the other hand, you are using a color composite monitor, a different Commodore socket will provide the output. In this case, a special composite video socket produces the video and audio signals for this type of monitor.

Finally, a joystick can be added to your JET flight system. This is an unnecessary item that is best avoided. Basically, the large number of keyboard-based instrument controls makes joystick flight impractical. Switching one's hands back and forth between the joystick and keyboard is an unwanted distraction in an already congested environment. If you feel that the realism of joystick control surface operation is vital to your enjoyment of JET, then plug one joystick into the Commodore's control port 1.

Starting JET on the Commodore 64/128 is a simple three-step procedure:

1. Turn on your Commodore system. (Commodore 128 owners will need to enter the C-64

mode before performing the next step. To do this type: GO64 at the READY prompt.)

2. Place the JET floppy disk in the disk drive and close the door.
3. Type the following command:

LOAD ''*'',8,1

and press the Return key.

Once the program has been loaded, you are presented with a menu for determining the type of monitor that you are using.

A Commodore system with a color monitor:
Press 1.
A Commodore system with a black and white monitor:
Press 2.
Your Commodore system is now ready for jet flight.

IBM. An enormous variety of different hardware products can be used with complete success on the IBM PC computer. This includes the IBM PC, PC XT, PC AT, and PCjr models. Essentially, these IBM computers must have a minimum of 128K bytes of RAM (random access memory), a graphics card, and a monitor. A joystick can be used optionally for control over the aircraft's three axes of movement.

One question that is bound to pop up concerns the use of JET with IBM PC compatible computers. Theoretically, every computer that sports a high degree of compatibility should run JET without any problems. As to actual tests, I have evaluated three different brands: Compaq, Heath/Zenith, and Tandy. All three of these manufacturers' products flew JET without fault. This statement isn't intended to serve as an endorsement, but rather a yardstick for you to use in your own compatibility tests.

The minimal memory requirement of 128K bytes of RAM shouldn't pose a problem to any of the IBM models (and other compatibles, for that matter). There is a degree of dissatisfaction, however, among IBM PC computer owners who have hard disk drives in their systems. This dissent arises from the JET copy protection scheme. Many of these users wish that they could install JET on their hard disk drives. Unfortunately, subLOGIC neglected to allow for such a provision. If hard disk drive installation is a desire of yours, there is a special program available from TranSec Systems, Inc. (1802-200 North University Drive, Plantation, FL 33322 (305) 474-7548; ask for Twin-Pak #201) that removes the copy protection from JET. The result is a non-copy-protected disk that can be installed on any hard disk drive or RAM disk drive.

There are three basic types of graphics cards that can be used with JET: the IBM Color/Graphics Monitor Adapter, the Hercules Graphics Card, and the IBM Enhanced Graphics Adapter. Of course, there is a vast assortment of cards and adapters that match the standards established by these three products. For example, the Paradise Modular Graphics Card, the AST Preview!, and the Tecmar EGA Master all duplicate the respective features of the three JET standards. Once again, only these three graphics card substitutes have been actually tested for JET compatibility. Other brands and models might not provide a sufficient degree of compatibility.

After the proper graphics card has been installed, only a monitor is required to complete the flight simulation system. In order to obtain the highest amount of image resolution, the IBM Monochrome Display, IBM Color Display, or the IBM Enhanced Color Display should be used with the appropriate graphics card (this includes all comparable monitors). Composite monitors and TV sets, while they will work, should be avoided due to their lower screen resolution.

One final item that can be added to your JET flight system is a joystick. This is an unnecessary option that should be avoided. Basically, the large number of keyboard-based instrument controls makes joystick flight impractical. Switching one's hands back and forth between the joystick and keyboard is an unwanted distraction in an already congested environment. Conversely, a quality joystick like CH Products' Mach III could actually improve your JET performance. If you feel that the realism of joystick control surface operation is vital to your enjoyment of JET, then plug one joystick into an IBM game port (on the IBM PCjr use the joystick 1 port). A special game port interface card must be used for the connection of the joystick. The Quadram Expanded Quadboard is an example of a card that has a game port interface.

Starting JET on an IBM PC computer is a simple two-step procedure:

1. Place the JET floppy disk in disk drive A and close the door.
2. Turn on your IBM PC computer.

JET can also be booted from a previously started IBM PC by simultaneously pressing the Ctrl + Alt + Del key combination.

There are several optional methods for starting JET which implement all of the different graphics card options.

1. Load PC-DOS.
For a Hercules Graphics Card system:

2a. From the DOS prompt, type:

A>JET H

and press the Enter key.
For an IBM EGA monochrome system:

2b. From the DOS prompt, type:

A>JET M

and press the Enter key.
For an IBM EGA color system:

2c. From the DOS prompt, type:

A>JET E

and press the Enter key.
For non-copy-protected hard disk drive systems:

2d. From the DOS prompt, type:

C>JET

and press the Enter key.
Hard disk drive users can also use one of the other graphics card/monitor starting commands.

Once the program has been loaded, you are presented with two menus for determining the nature of the keyboard and the type of monitor that you are using.

The keyboard menu—
Use an optional joystick:
Press J.
An IBM PC (e.g., PC, PC XT,and PC AT) system:

Press 1.
An IBM PCjr system:
Press 2.
The monitor menú—
An IBM PC system with a composite, TV, or monochrome monitor:
Press 1.
An IBM PC system with an RGB monitor:
Press 2.
An IBM PCjr system with a PCjr RGB monitor:
Press 3.
Your IBM system is now ready for jet flight.

THE COMPUTER COCKPIT

No matter which computer version of JET you are flying, the operation of the controls and the representation of the instruments remains the same.

The HUD. All of the jet fighter's instrumentation and current flight status is displayed on the computer system's monitor. The format of the monitor's screen closely approximates the amount of information that is contained on a contemporary jet aircraft's head-up display or HUD (the JET Operating Manual erroneously defines the HUD as a heads-up display). Figure 1-11 shows

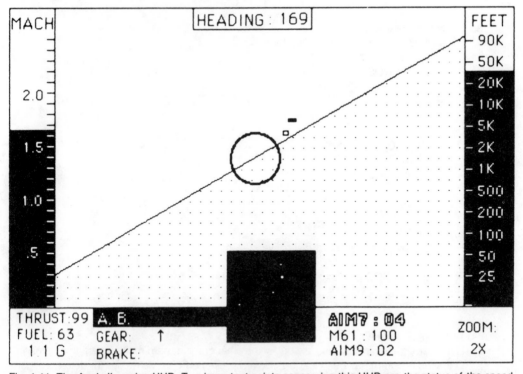

Fig. 1-11. The Apple II version HUD. Two important points concerning this HUD are the status of the speed brake and the designation of an active system. When the speed brake is engaged, a small box will appear next to the BRAKE: instrument on the HUD. The currently active weapon system, on the other hand, will move to the top of the weapon's list and be highlighted in red. This same highlighting technique is also used when the afterburner is engaged.

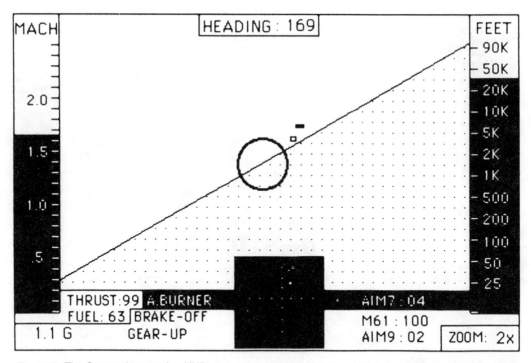

Fig. 1-12. The Commodore version HUD. An enemy jet (the black square) has just fired a missile (the white square) at your aircraft. Furthermore, the black Weapon Tracking Indicator states that the target is within range for firing the AIM-7 weapon system.

the HUD on an Apple II computer system. The Commodore 64/128 computer system's HUD is represented in Fig. 1-12. An IBM PC HUD is illustrated in Fig. 1-13. Refer to your respective computer's HUD figure during the explanation of the remaining JET controls and instruments.

Heading Indicator—The aircraft's current direction is displayed as a magnetic heading in compass degrees.

Altimeter—A vertical bar scale that shows the aircraft's altitude in feet above ground level.

View Magnification—Four factors of perspective alter the pilot's angle of view.

Landing Gear Status Indicator—Displays whether the landing gear is extended or retracted. (The IBM version uses a highlight to indicate that the landing gear is extended and no highlight to show when the gear is retracted.)

Speed Brake Status Indicator—Displays whether the speed brake is extended or retracted. (The IBM version uses a highlight to indicate that the speed brake is extended and no highlight to show when the speed brake is retracted.)

Fuel Quantity Indicator—A constant readout of the percentage of fuel that is remaining in the aircraft's internal fuel tanks.

Weapon Status—A numeric value indicating the quantity of ordnance remaining for the currently active weapon.

Weapon System Select—Shows the currently active weapon system. (The Commodore version uses a highlight to indicate the currently active weapon system.)

Afterburner Status Indicator—Uses a highlight to indicate when the afterburners have been engaged. No highlight represents disengaged afterburners.

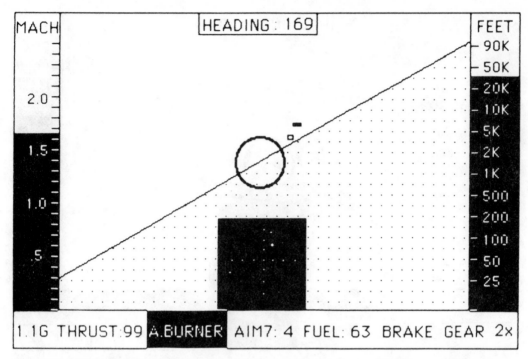

Fig. 1-13. The IBM PC version HUD. Inverse fields are used to represent active systems. In this example, the engaged afterburner is indicated by the inverse box surrounding the A.BURNER instrument.

Engine Thrust Indicator—Displays the percentage of thrust being produced by the aircraft's jet engine.

Frame Loading Indicator—Measures the number of Gs being applied to the aircraft. One G is equal to the force of gravity on an object when at rest.

Airspeed Indicator—A vertical bar scale that gives the true airspeed of the aircraft in a Mach number.

Several of these instruments share a unique range of values.

Heading Indicator—0 to 359 degrees, where 0 degrees is north and 180 degrees is south.

Altimeter—0 to 90,000 feet; a ''K'' represents × 1000. Therefore, 5K equals 5,000 feet.

View Magnification—1 to 8 ×; 2 × is considered a normal view.

Fuel Quantity Indicator—0 to 99 percent.

Weapon Status—0 to 6 for all external store ordnance; 0 to 500 rounds for the M61A1 cannon.

Weapon System Select—AGM-65E Maverick, MK-82 LD/HD/LGB, and M61A1 for ground attack; AIM-9G/H/L, AIM-7F, and M61A1 for air-to-air combat.

Engine Thrust Indicator—0 to 99 percent; the afterburners are automatically engaged when thrust is 99 percent plus.

Frame Loading Indicator— − 3 to 9Gs; at − 3Gs the pilot will ''red out'' and at 9Gs the pilot will ''black out.''

Airspeed Indicator—0 to 2.0 Mach.

Instrument Selection. There are three instruments that can be alternately engaged and disengaged at the pilot's discretion.

Radar System Display—A multimode Doppler radar system used for target selection, enemy missile avoidance, and all-aspect view coverage.

Operation: An active Radar System Display shows all enemy targets as red dots (these are gray dots on the IBM version). A flashing red dot is used to indicate the selected target. Enemy missiles are moving white dots on the display screen. This instrument should always be used during a combat mission.

Weapon Tracking Indicator—Calculates the selected target's distance with reference to the range of the active weapon system.

Operation: A white circle indicates that the selected target is out of range. When the circle turns black, the target is within the range of the selected weapon system. As you close on the target, the black circle will change to white in a counterclockwise fashion. This instrument should always be used during any form of jet flight.

Attitude Indicator—A moving scale that shows the current pitch and roll attitude of the aircraft.

Operation: A scale of horizontal lines spaced at 20 degree intervals moves as you pitch, roll, or bank your aircraft. The exact number of degrees that the aircraft is either pitched up or pitched down can be determined by reading the Attitude Indicator as it intersects the Weapon Tracking Indicator circle. Exact roll and bank values are not provided by this instrument. Only a rough visual approximation can be obtained from its use. This instrument is of a questionable value. Learn to fly without it and you will never need it.

Aircraft Controls. The actual flying of JET is performed by six controls.

Elevator—Controls the pitch movement of the aircraft.

Operation: Neutralizing the controls will halt the aircraft's pitch rotation. The optional joystick operates this control.

Ailerons and Rudder—Controls the roll and bank movement of the aircraft.

Operation: A roll is produced by constantly holding either a left or right aileron and rudder combination. Neutralizing the controls will halt the aircraft's roll and bank rotation. The optional joystick operates this control.

Throttle—Increases or decreases the amount of thrust generated by the jet engine. This control also engages and disengages the afterburner.

Operation: A sustained holding of either the increase or decrease throttle key will continuously raise or lower the amount of engine thrust.

Speed Brake—Dramatically reduces the airspeed of the aircraft.

Landing Gear—Used for landing the aircraft and subsequent taxi control.

Emergency Escape System—This is a final action. When all is lost, bail out of the aircraft.

Visual Orientation. Good pilot visibility is the key to successful jet flight. There are two different viewpoint modes and five different view directions.

Pilot Mode—A view from the jet aircraft's cockpit.

Control Tower Mode—A view from the control tower of the aircraft's home base (or home aircraft carrier, in the case of flying the F/A-18 carrier-based aircraft).

Forward View—Looking straight ahead, out the front of the canopy.

Backward View—Looking over the pilot's shoulder, out the rear of the canopy.

Upward View—Looking straight up, out the top of the canopy.

Right View—Looking out the right side of the cockpit.

Left View—Looking out the left side of the cockpit.

In both of the viewpoint modes and in all of the view directions, the view magnification can be altered to suit the needs of a particular visual situation.

Miscellaneous Controls. There are four remaining JET controls that serve as system maintenance features.

Pause—Stops all of the JET action so that you can catch your breath or plot a strategy. (The Apple version also has a ''pause with message'' feature.)

Sound—Turns the sound effects on or off.

Exit JET—Stops the current flight simulation and returns to the main startup menus.

Center the Screen (This is only found on the IBM version.)—centers the JET image on the monitor's screen.

Joystick (This is only found on the Apple version.)—Enables and centers or disables the joystick.

Reload Scenery Data Base (This is only found on the Apple version.)—Updates the screen with a new scenery disk when a data base boundary is crossed.

Chapter 2

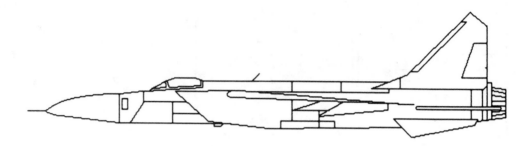

Orientation Flight

The best way to become familiar with the function of the numerous jet aircraft controls is to take JET up for a quick "hands-off" test flight. This initial flight will only cover a minimal amount of instructional material. Basically, you will just take off, level the aircraft at a shallow altitude, turn back toward the base, and land. Remarkably, this entire flight is visually contained on the following pages. Therefore, JET doesn't even need to be booted for this initial flight.

Another important facet of the flight instruction that is provided in this chapter deals with the manner of its presentation. This material shares the same format that will be used for conducting all of the historical aviation scenarios that are detailed in Part II of this book. Don't slough over the importance of learning this instructional method at this early stage. Only when you thoroughly understand this format will you then be able to concentrate on perfecting your flying technique.

F-16 ORIENTATION FLIGHT

Use the appropriate JET starting method as discussed in Chapter 1. With the initial computer-oriented menu(s) correctly answered, begin the orientation flight setup.

Setup.
Select Game Mode.
Press 3.
Choose Skill Level.
Press 0.
Select Aircraft Type.
Press 2.

Mission Objectives. Your goal during this flight is to successfully follow a 15-step orientation flight.

Flying the Mission. Figure 2-1 is an aerial view of your base. Your F-16 is sitting inside a hangar. Your heading is 270 degrees (facing due west). The fuel reading is 99 percent and the thrust is at 0 percent. There is 1.0G of gravitational pressure on the aircraft. You have a forward

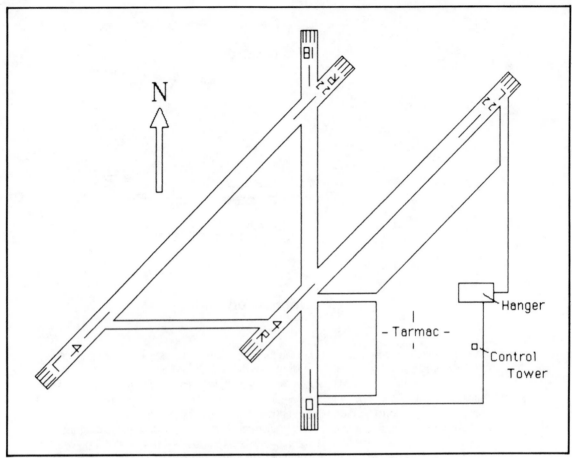

Fig. 2-1. An aerial map of the F-16 airfield.

view with a view magnification of 2×. At this time, activate the Weapon Tracking Indicator. This circle will be useful in achieving the correct aircraft attitude during flight. Of course, you could also use the Attitude Indicator, but this is more of a nuisance than an aid.

Step 1. Increase throttle to 4 percent. Begin your taxi roll (Fig. 2-2).

Step 2. When you have cleared the hangar, turn left to a new heading of 180 degrees (Fig. 2-3).

Step 3. Taxi to the end of the tarmac and turn to a heading of 270 degrees (Fig. 2-4).

Step 4. Taxi onto runway 0 and take a final ground heading of 0 degrees (Fig. 2-5).

Step 5. Begin takeoff roll. Increase throttle to 99 percent, then engage the afterburner (Fig. 2-6).

Step 6. When your airspeed reaches Mach .3, give a slight up elevator with two up elevator keystrokes. Neutralize your pitch (Fig. 2-7).

Step 7. At an altitude of 100 feet and an airspeed of Mach .45, raise your landing gear (Fig. 2-8).

Step 8. When you reach an altitude of 500 feet, decrease throttle to 49 percent and give a slight down elevator with two down elevator keystrokes. Neutralize the pitch when the aircraft is level (Fig. 2-9).

Step 9. Your airspeed should now read Mach .775 with the altimeter reading 1K. The throt-

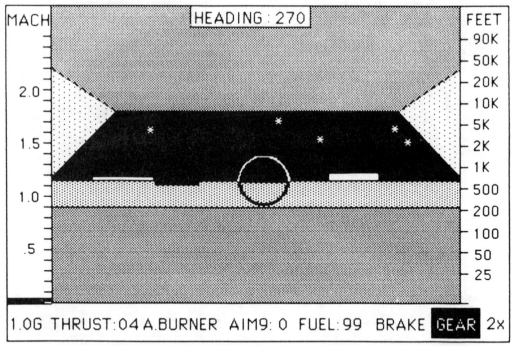

Fig. 2-2. Applying a modest amount of thrust moves the F-16 out of its hangar. (*Note:* some of the values displayed in the following illustrations might differ between the various JET versions.

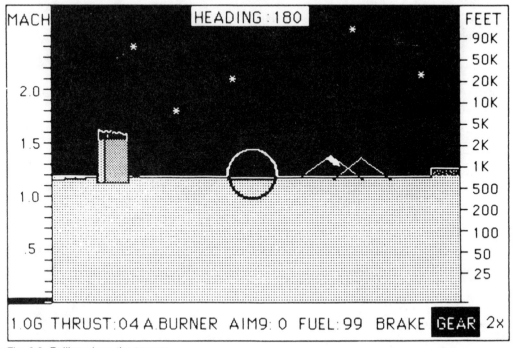

Fig. 2-3. Rolling along the tarmac.

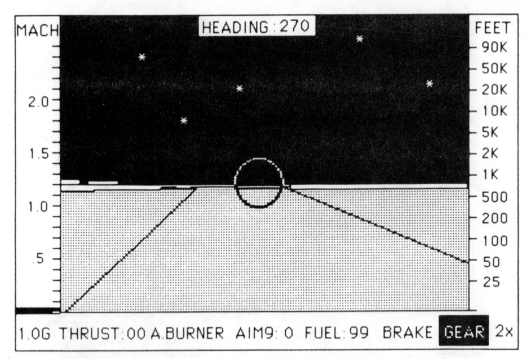

MACH   HEADING:270   FEET

1.0G THRUST:00 A.BURNER AIM9:0 FUEL:99 BRAKE GEAR 2x

Fig. 2-4. Entering the runway ramp.

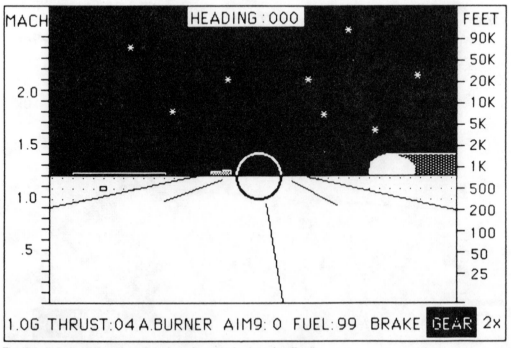

MACH   HEADING:000   FEET

1.0G THRUST:04 A.BURNER AIM9:0 FUEL:99 BRAKE GEAR 2x

Fig. 2-5. Lined up on runway 0 and ready to begin the takeoff roll.

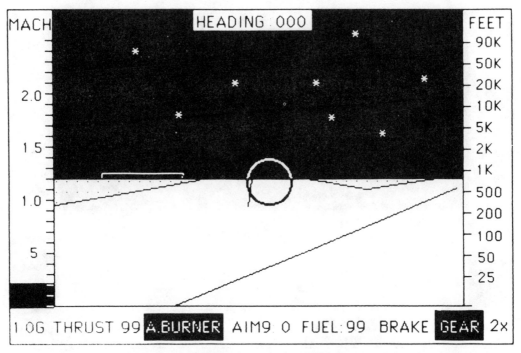

Fig. 2-6. The afterburner has been engaged and your jet is accelerating.

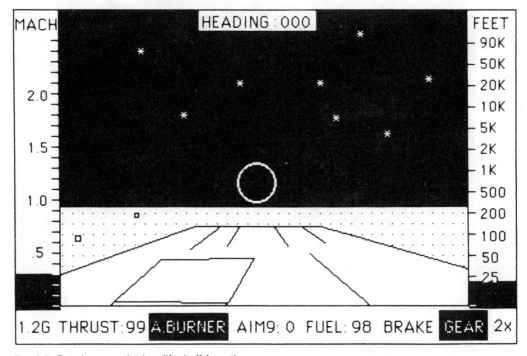

Fig. 2-7. Rotation; your jet has lifted off from the runway.

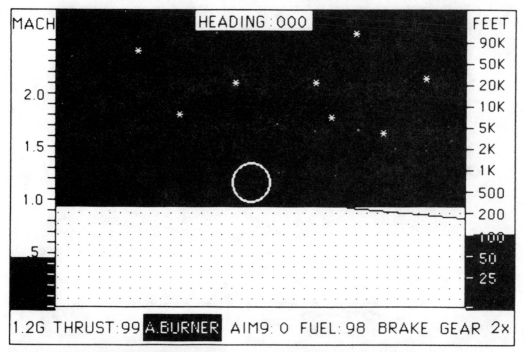

Fig. 2-8. The landing gear has been retracted and you are climbing away from the ground.

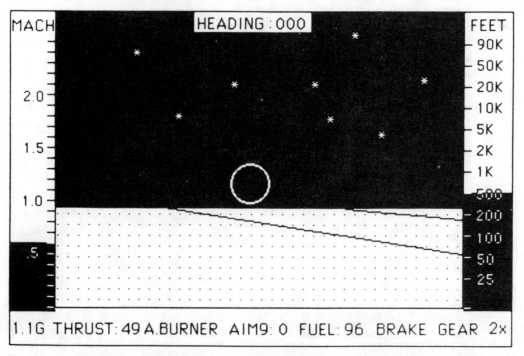

Fig. 2-9. You continue to climb even following the disengagement of the afterburner.

tle should still be set at 49 percent and there should be about 95 percent of your fuel remaining (Fig. 2-10).

Step 10. Place the aircraft in a steep 45 degree bank to the right. Neutralize the bank. You will see your airspeed and altitude decrease, while the heading and frame loading increase (Fig. 2-11).

Step 11. With a heading of 185 degrees, decrease the angle of bank to 5 degrees and decrease throttle to 19 percent (Fig. 2-12).

Step 12. Level the aircraft at a heading of 220 by banking left and then neutralizing the bank (Fig. 2-13).

Step 13. Lower the landing gear and engage the speed brake (Fig. 2-14).

Step 14. Line up on runway 220. Give some down elevator until the aircraft's nose is pointing at the far end of the runway (Fig. 2-15).

Step 15. Reduce the throttle to 9 percent and begin raising the nose of the aircraft slightly with some up elevator. Touch down. Exit the runway to the tarmac and taxi into the hangar (Fig. 2-16).

Mission Debriefing. If you successfully completed the following maneuvers, then you will have a passing grade for this mission:

☐ Taxi the aircraft on the tarmac.
☐ Take off on the described compass heading.
☐ Level the aircraft at 1000 feet.
☐ Complete a 45 degree bank to the right.
☐ Land the aircraft on the specified runway.
☐ Taxi into the hangar.

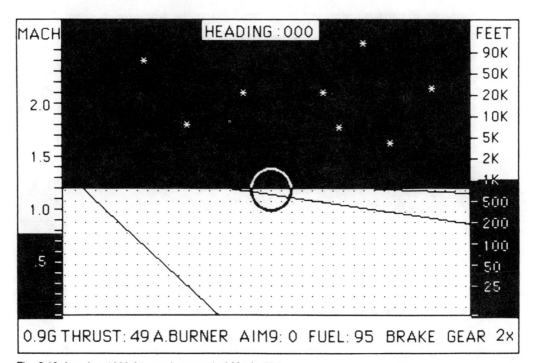

Fig. 2-10. Level at 1000 feet and a speed of Mach .775.

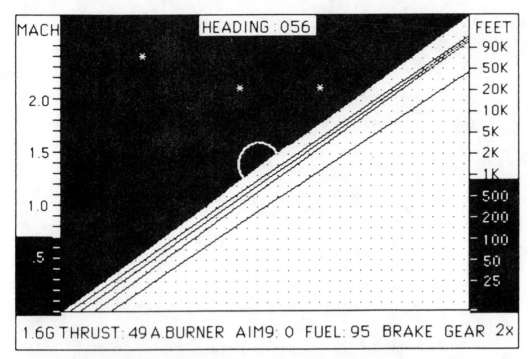

Fig. 2-11. A steep 45-degree turn to the right.

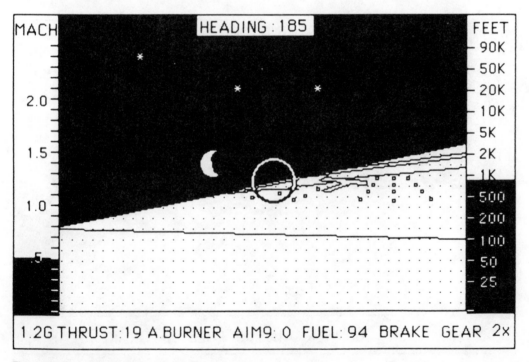

Fig. 2-12. The airfield is becoming visible.

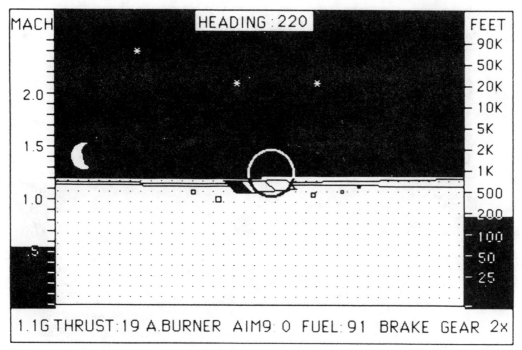

Fig. 2-13. Leveling the aircraft on a steady heading of 220.

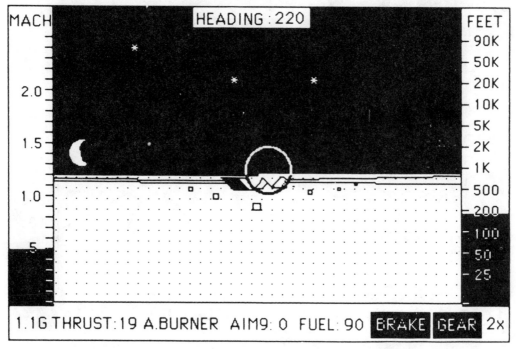

Fig. 2-14. Extend the landing gear and engage the speed brake.

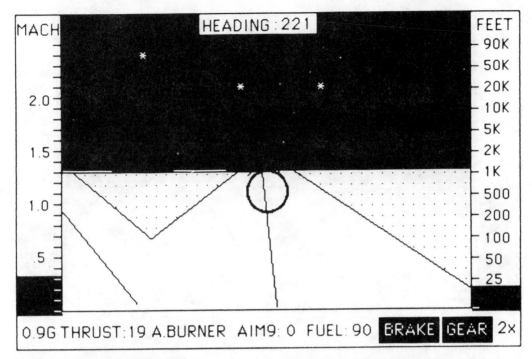

Fig. 2-15. Lined up on runway 220.

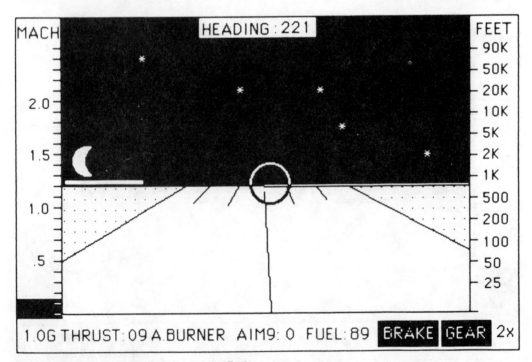

Fig. 2-16. You have successfully landed the F-16.

F/A-18 ORIENTATION FLIGHT

Use the appropriate JET starting method as discussed in Chapter 1. With the initial computer-oriented menu(s) correctly answered, begin the orientation flight setup.

Setup.

Select Game Mode.

Press 3.

Choose Skill Level.

Press 0.

Select Aircraft Type.

Press 1.

Mission Objectives. Your goal during this flight is to successfully follow a 15-step orientation flight.

Flying the Mission. Figure 2-17 is an aerial view of your home aircraft carrier. At this time, your F/A-18 is sitting on the flight deck of the aircraft carrier. Your F/A-18 is engaged with the carrier's catapult. Your heading is 90 degrees (facing due east). The fuel reading is 99 percent and the thrust is at 0 percent. There is 1.0G of gravitational pressure on the aircraft. You have a forward view with a view magnification of 2 x. At this time activate the Weapon Tracking Indicator. This circle will be useful in achieving the correct aircraft attitude during flight. Of course, you could also use the Attitude Indicator, but this is more of a nuisance than an aid.

Step 1. Increase throttle to 99 percent and engage the afterburners (Fig. 2-18).

Step 2. Press the L key to activate the catapult launch system (Fig. 2-19).

Step 3. When your airspeed reaches Mach .3, give a slight up elevator with two up elevator keystrokes. Neutralize your pitch (Fig. 2-20).

Step 4. At an altitude of 100 feet and an airspeed of Mach .45, raise your landing gear (Fig. 2-21).

Step 5. When you reach an altitude of 500 feet, decrease throttle to 49 percent and give a slight down elevator with two down elevator keystrokes. Neutralize the pitch when the aircraft is level (Fig. 2-22).

Step 6. Your airspeed should now read Mach .650 with the altimeter reading 1K. The throttle should still be set at 49 percent and the heading is 90 degrees (Fig. 2-23).

Step 7. Place the aircraft in a steep 45 degree bank to the left. Neutralize the bank. Level the aircraft when the heading is 0 degrees. You will see your airspeed, altitude, and heading decrease, while the frame loading increases (Fig. 2-24).

Step 8. Place the aircraft in another steep 45 degree bank to the left. Neutralize the bank. Level the aircraft when the heading is 270 degrees. Your airspeed should be Mach .725 with an altitude of 600 feet (Fig. 2-25).

Step 9. Raise the aircraft's nose and climb back to an altitude of 1000 feet. Switch View Magnification to 1 x. Change the pilot's view to a left view (Fig. 2-26).

Step 10. Locate your aircraft carrier. Fly three miles west of the carrier. Each of the lines on the water's surface represents one mile and the current compass heading is due west (i.e., 270 degrees) (Fig. 2-27).

Step 11. At three miles west of the carrier, bank left at 45 degrees. Neutralize the bank and level the aircraft on a heading of 180 degrees. The airspeed should be Mach .8 with an altitude of 700 feet (Fig. 2-28).

Step 12. Switch to a conning tower viewpoint (Fig. 2-29).

Step 13. When the plane-handling crane becomes visible on the left side of the carrier, switch back to a forward pilot viewpoint. Bank left to a new heading of 90 degrees. Reduce throttle to 19 percent and lower the landing gear (Fig. 2-30).

Step 14. Line up on the carrier's landing deck. Lower the aircraft's nose with a slight amount of down elevator. Point the nose at the bow of the carrier (Fig. 2-31).

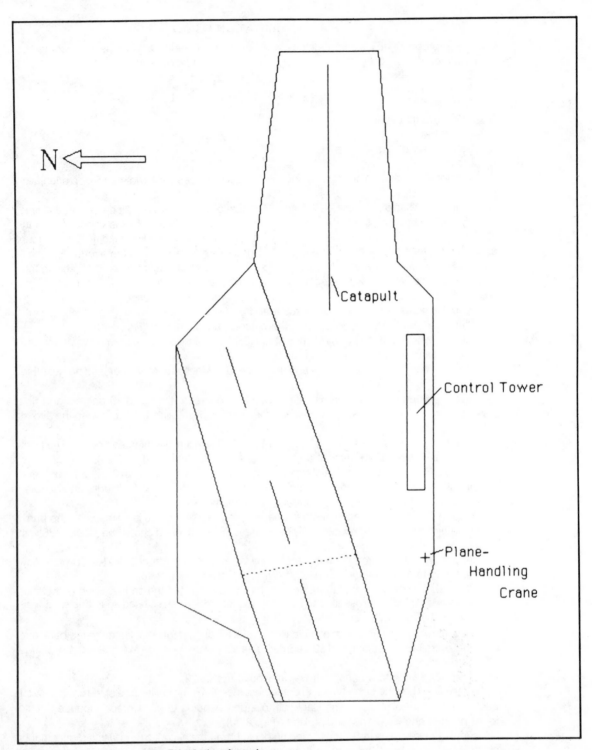

N

Catapult

Control Tower

+ Plane-
Handling
Crane

Fig. 2-17. An aerial view of the F/A-18 aircraft carrier.

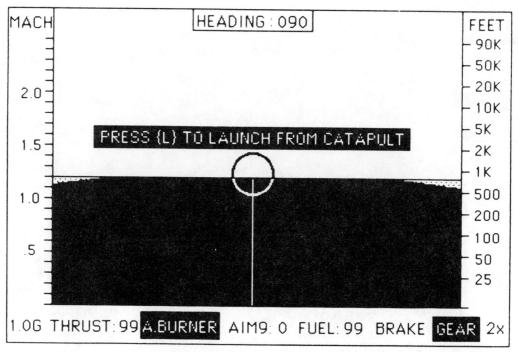

Fig. 2-18. Engage the afterburner and prepare to launch from the catapult.

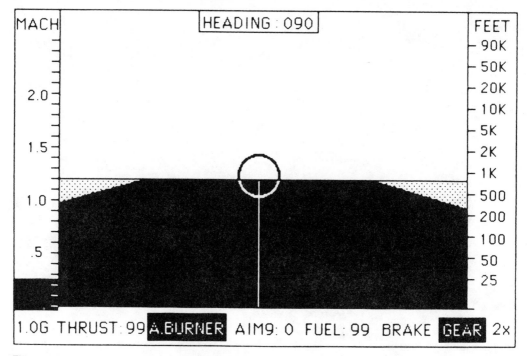

Fig. 2-19. Press L and your F/A-18 begins to accelerate.

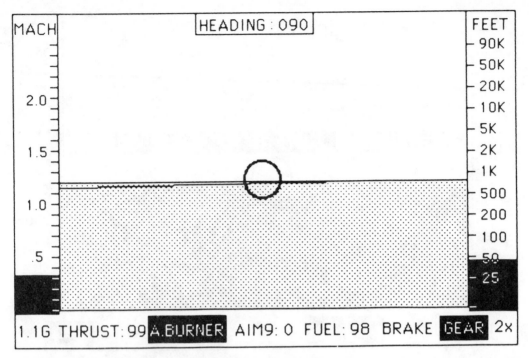

Fig. 2-20. As you leave the carrier, give a slight amount of up pitch.

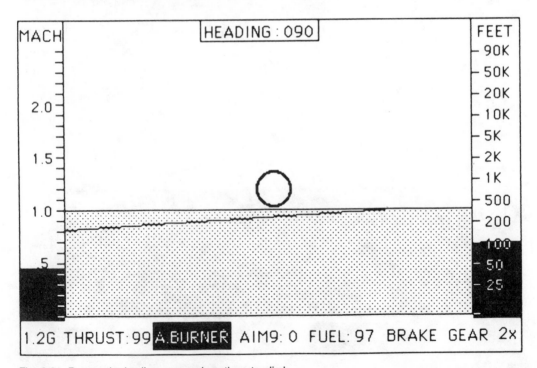

Fig. 2-21. Retract the landing gear and continue to climb.

40

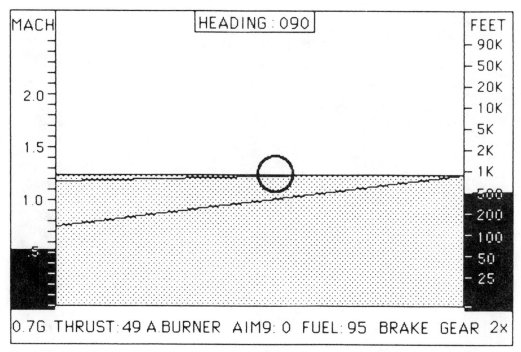

HEADING : 090

FEET

90K
50K
20K
10K
5K
2K
1K
500
200
100
50
25

2.0

1.5

1.0

.5

0.7G THRUST:49 A.BURNER AIM9: 0 FUEL: 95 BRAKE GEAR 2x

Fig. 2-22. At an altitude of 500 feet, disengage the afterburner and reduce the throttle to 49 percent.

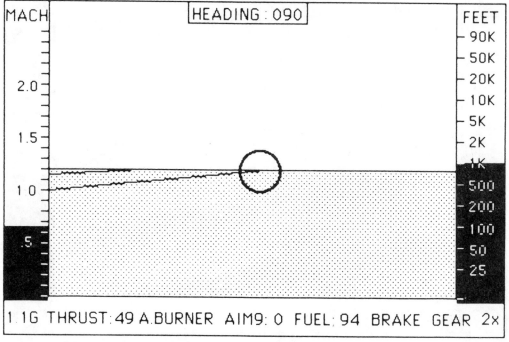

MACH

HEADING : 090

FEET

90K
50K
20K
10K
5K
2K
1K
500
200
100
50
25

2.0

1.5

1.0

.5

1.1G THRUST:49 A.BURNER AIM9: 0 FUEL:94 BRAKE GEAR 2x

Fig. 2-23. Level your F/A-18 at 1000 feet.

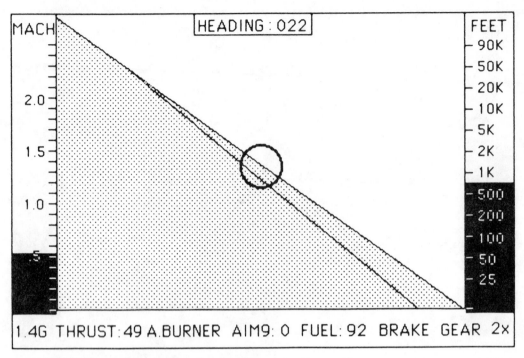

Fig. 2-24. Execute a steep 45-degree turn to the left.

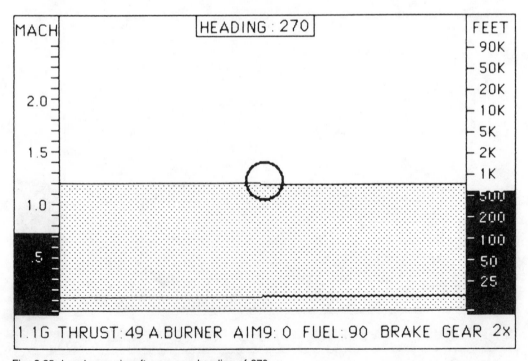

Fig. 2-25. Level your aircraft on a new heading of 270.

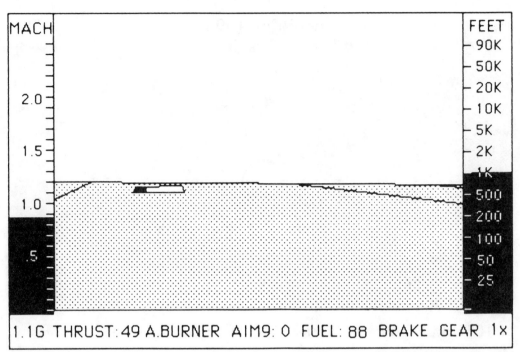

MACH		FEET

1.1G THRUST:49 A.BURNER AIM9:0 FUEL:88 BRAKE GEAR 1x

Fig. 2-26. Turn your head for a left view and reduce your View Magnification to 1 x. That's your aircraft carrier in the distance.

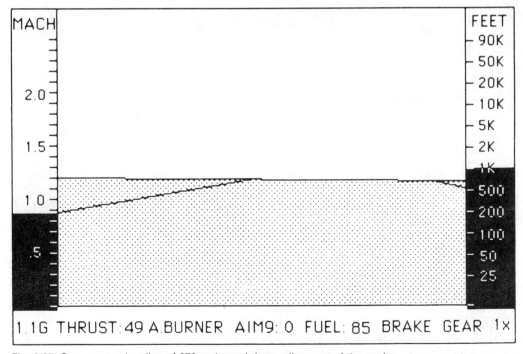

1.1G THRUST:49 A.BURNER AIM9:0 FUEL:85 BRAKE GEAR 1x

Fig. 2-27. Stay on your heading of 270 and travel three miles west of the carrier.

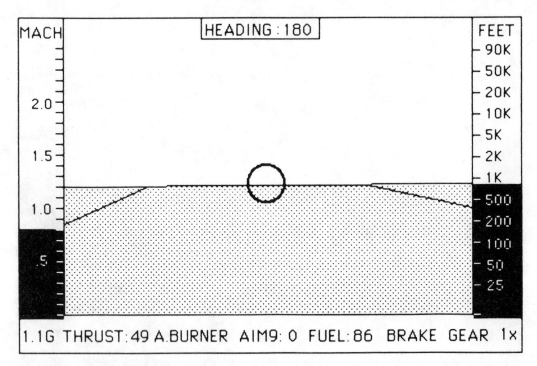

Fig. 2-28. Turn left to a new heading of 180.

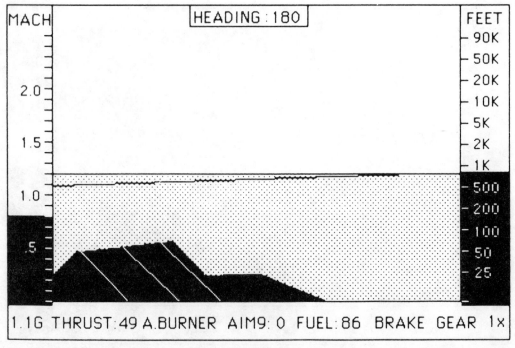

Fig. 2-29. Switch to a conning tower viewpoint. Remember to stay at a View Magnification of 1×.

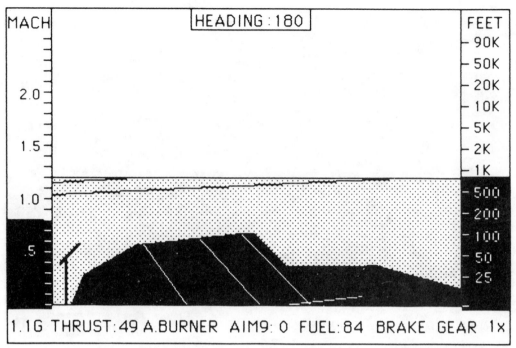

Fig. 2-30. When the plane-handling crane becomes visible along the left of the conning tower viewpoint, return to the pilot's viewpoint and execute a left turn to a heading of 90.

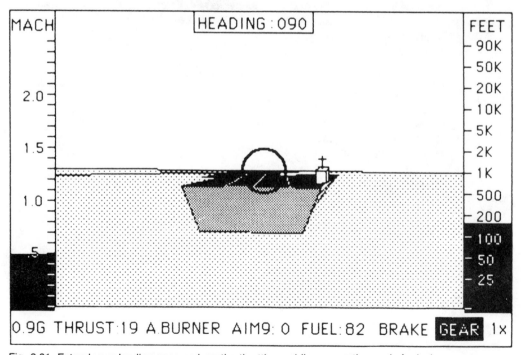

Fig. 2-31. Extend your landing gear, reduce the throttle, and line up on the carrier's deck.

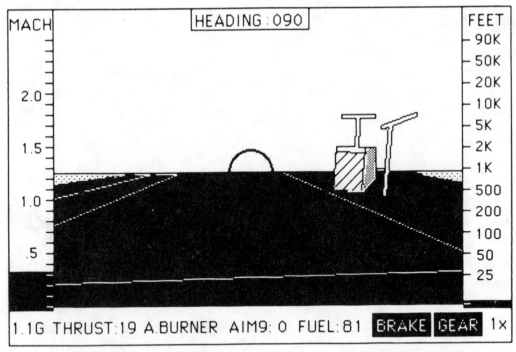

MACH	HEADING:090	FEET

2.0		— 90K
		— 50K
		— 20K
		— 10K
1.5		— 5K
		— 2K
		— 1K
1.0		— 500
		— 200
		— 100
.5		— 50
		— 25

1.1G THRUST:19 A.BURNER AIM9: O FUEL:81 BRAKE GEAR 1×

Fig. 2-32. Engage the speed brake and slowly settle your F/A-18 onto the carrier's deck.

Step 15. Engage the speed brake and clear the stern of the carrier (this is approximately 50 feet high). Raise the aircraft's nose slightly and engage the arresting cable (Fig. 2-32).

Mission Debriefing. If you successfully completed the following maneuvers, then you will have a passing grade for this mission:

☐ Launch the aircraft from the carrier.
☐ Take off on the described compass heading.
☐ Level the aircraft at 1000 feet.
☐ Complete a series of 45 degree banks to the left.
☐ Land the aircraft on the carrier deck.
☐ Engage the arresting cable.

Now that you've had a taste of high-speed jet performance, it's time for a more extensive course in flight instruction.

Chapter 3

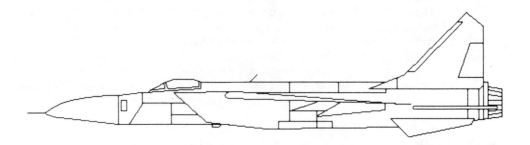

Flight Instruction

Learning the intricacies of jet flight can be an exacting process. Each flight—or, more likely, flight *attempt*—is fraught with potential aircraft and pilot disaster. All of these physical stresses and structural excesses are unnecessary. By using a planned and patient instructional technique, all of the JET functions can be mastered in just four simple lessons.

These lessons take you from your beginning efforts at learning how to taxi the F-16 around on the ground to recovering from a high-altitude, high-speed stall condition in the F/A-18. Each lesson is complete with a step-by-step guide for learning how to perform the particular flight maneuver. This step-by-step process can be repeated as many times as needed for gaining the degree of proficiency that is required for becoming a jet pilot. At the conclusion of each lesson a competence test will evaluate your mastery of the instruction that has been presented in that particular lesson. Therefore, if you can pass all four lesson tests, then you will have absolutely no problem successfully soloing in the next chapter.

Setup. The initial menu setup will be the same for all four of these lessons.

Select Game Mode.

Press 3.

Choose Skill Level.

Press 0.

LESSON 1

F-16 Setup. If at any point during this lesson you crash the aircraft, just exit JET and return to the setup menus.

Select Aircraft Type.

Press 2.

Lesson Objectives. Learn to taxi, take off, and land the F-16.

Performing the Lesson. In order to have a reference "spot" on the forward canopy view, engage the Weapon Tracking Indicator. You are starting inside the home base hangar with a heading of 270 degrees and 0 percent thrust.

Taxi:

Step 1. Apply 4 percent thrust. Watch the airspeed indicator. As you start to move, you will leave the hangar.

Step 2. When you have cleared the hangar, make a hard left turn to a new heading of 180 degrees. Hold the left turn key down until you reach the new heading, then neutralize the turn.

Step 3. The F-16 is now skidding to the right. Even though the aircraft's nose is pointed to a heading of 180 degrees, the entire aircraft is skidding to a heading of 270 degrees.

Step 4. Increase thrust to 14 percent. This forward thrust will slowly counteract the skid.

Step 5. When you are moving forward once again, decrease thrust to 0 percent.

Step 6. Taxi to a heading of 0 degrees by making a slower turn. If necessary, apply increased thrust to reduce any tendency to skid. After any thrust increase, always reduce thrust back to 0 percent.

Step 7. Engage the speed brake. Slowly taxi back inside the hangar.

Three important points to remember when taxiing the F-16: use slow speeds, keep the thrust to a minimum, and make all of your turns wide. If you do get into a ground skid, however, just apply a modest increase in thrust.

Taxi Test. Taxi the F-16 along all three of the runways at the home base and return to the hangar. You will receive a passing grade on this test if you can:

☐ Travel all three of the runways.
☐ Avoid skidding the aircraft.

Take Off.

Step 1. Taxi out of the hangar and onto runway 22L.

Step 2. Slowly taxi the entire length of the runway at a reduced throttle of 4 percent thrust. Study the various landmarks along the length of the runway.

Step 3. Stop at the far end of the runway and turn to a new heading of 40 degrees. Keep the F-16 on the same runway that you just taxied down. This step might require the execution of a controlled skid.

Step 4. Begin the takeoff roll. Slowly increase the throttle. Engage the afterburner.

Step 5. As your airspeed reaches Mach .3, give some up elevator. Use two keystrokes of the up elevator key.

Step 6. When the nose of the F-16 clears the ground, neutralize the pitch (Fig. 3-1).

Step 7. Retract the landing gear and disengage the afterburner.

Takeoff Test. Use each runway and take off from each direction. You will receive a passing grade on this test if you can:

☐ Make a smooth and steady rate of climb during takeoff.
☐ Raise the landing gear.
☐ Cut the afterburner following the retraction of the landing gear.

Landing.

Step 1. Taxi to runway 4R.

Step 2. Turn to a heading of 40 degrees. Line up in the center of the runway.

Step 3. Begin takeoff roll. Increase throttle and engage afterburner.

Step 4. Give a slight amount of up elevator. Use two up elevator keystrokes.

Step 5. As the nose leaves the ground, neutralize the pitch. When you are airborne, retract the landing gear and disengage the afterburner.

Step 6. Reduce the throttle to 49 percent. Level the F-16 at an altitude of 1K, by using a slight down elevator.

Step 7. Bank 45 degrees to the left. Reduce the throttle to 19 percent while in the bank.

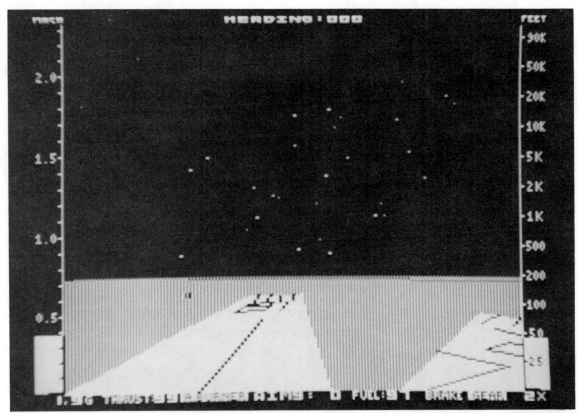
Fig. 3-1. Leaving runway 0 under maximum power.

Step 8. Level the aircraft at 180 degrees. Line up on runway 18. Use an increased View Magnification for making minor course adjustments.

Step 9. Lower the landing gear. Engage the speed brake.

Step 10. Give a slight down elevator. Use two down elevator keystrokes.

Step 11. At an altitude of 200 feet, start bringing the nose up with small amounts of up elevator and neutralize the pitch.

Step 12. Place the Target Tracking Indicator on a spot at the far end of the runway.

Step 13. Reduce throttle to 4 percent.

Step 14. At an altitude of 50 feet, start raising the aircraft's nose (Fig. 3-2). Use one press of the up elevator key and don't neutralize the pitch.

Step 15. Touch down.

Landing Test. Make a landing on all three runways, taxi off of each runway, and taxi into the hangar.

You will receive a passing grade on this test if you can:

☐ Line up on the proper runway.
☐ Reduce throttle for a slow approach.
☐ Lower the landing gear and engage the speed brake.
☐ Land on the runway.

F/A-18 Setup. If at any point during this lesson you crash the aircraft, just exit JET and return to the setup menus.

Select Aircraft Type.

Press 1.

Lesson Objectives. Learn to take off and land the F/A-18.

Performing the Lesson. In order to have a reference "spot" on the forward canopy view, engage the Weapon Tracking Indicator. You are starting on the deck of the home aircraft carrier with a heading of 90 degrees and 0 percent thrust.

Take Off.

Step 1. Slowly increase the throttle. Engage the afterburners.

Step 2. Launch the aircraft. Press the L key to activate the launch catapult.

Step 3. At an airspeed of Mach .3, give a slight amount of up elevator. Press the up elevator key twice.

Step 4. Clear the carrier and gain altitude. Neutralize the pitch.

Step 5. Retract landing gear.

Step 6. Disengage the afterburners.

Step 7. Use a Backward View and watch the aircraft carrier.

A peculiarity with the launch of the F/A-18 is that the up elevator pitch might not be recognized by the aircraft until after it clears the bow of the carrier. Therefore, if the F/A-18 fails to gain altitude immediately after launch, continue to apply up elevator until the aircraft begins to climb.

Takeoff Test. Take off from the aircraft carrier.

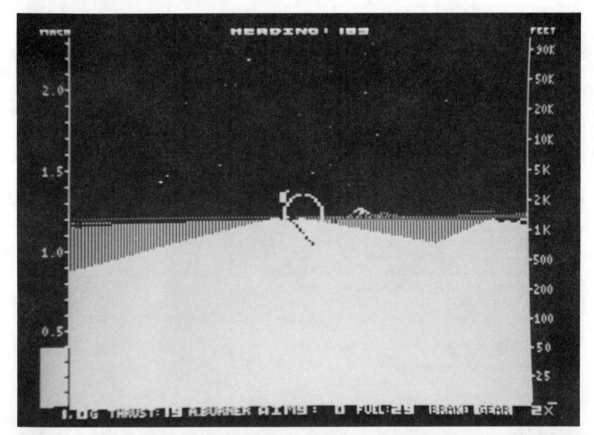

Fig. 3-2. A slow, steady descent is the key to a good landing. In this case, a low throttle setting and an engaged speed brake help to reduce the aircraft's speed.

You will receive a passing grade on this test if you can:

☐ Make a steady, smooth rate of climb after taking off.
☐ Raise the landing gear.
☐ Disengage the afterburners.

Landing.

Step 1. Use a standard aircraft carrier takeoff procedure.

Step 2. Raise the landing gear and disengage the afterburners after you clear the bow of the ship. Neutralize the pitch up.

Step 3. Reduce the throttle to 49 percent.

Step 4. Level the aircraft at an altitude of 1K with a slight amount of down elevator. Use two keystrokes of down elevator. Neutralize the down pitch at 1K.

Step 5. Bank 45 degrees to the left. Neutralize the bank. Level the aircraft when a heading of 0 degrees is achieved.

Step 6. Bank 45 degrees to the left again. Neutralize the bank. Level the aircraft on a heading of 270 degrees. Maintain an altitude of 1K. A slight pitch upward might be necessary to keep the aircraft at this altitude.

Step 7. Switch to a View Magnification of 1 x and use a Left View. Continue to use this magnification for the remainder of this lesson.

Step 8. Fly three miles west of the carrier. Each line on the water's surface represents one mile. Switch the viewpoint back to the Pilot Mode.

Fig. 3-3. Closing in on the carrier's deck and the arresting cable.

Step 9. Bank 45 degrees to the left. Neutralize the bank and level the aircraft on a heading of 180 degrees.

Step 10. Switch the viewpoint to the Control Tower Mode. When the plane-handling crane becomes visible on the left side of the carrier, switch the viewpoint back to the Pilot Mode.

Step 11. Bank left to a new heading of 90 degrees. Reduce throttle to 19 percent. Lower the landing gear.

Step 12. Line up with the carrier's landing deck. Increasing the View Magnification will help with this function. Return the View Magnification to 1 × for the actual landing. Lower the F/A-18's nose with a slight amount of down elevator. Place the Weapon Tracking Indicator on a point near the bow of the carrier.

Step 13. Engage the speed brake and clear the stern of the ship (Fig. 3-3). Raise the nose of the aircraft slightly and engage the arresting cable.

Step 14. Touch down.

Landing Test. Land on the carrier's landing deck.
You will receive a passing grade on this test if you can:

☐ Line up on the carrier's landing deck.
☐ Make a slow approach.
☐ Lower the landing gear.
☐ Engage the arresting cable.

LESSON 2

Lesson Setup. If at any point during this lesson you crash the aircraft, just exit JET and return to the setup menus.

Select Aircraft Type.
Press 1 for F/A-18 practice.
Press 2 for F-16 practice.

Lesson Objectives. Learn to change altitude and alter airspeed in the F/A-18 and the F-16.

Performing the Lesson. In order to have a reference ''spot'' on the forward canopy view, engage the Weapon Tracking Indicator.

Altitude Change.
Step 1. Take off.

Step 2. Keep the afterburner engaged and retract the landing gear.

Step 3. Continue to climb to an altitude of 10K. The rate of climb should be both slow and steady.

Step 4. At an altitude of 10K, disengage the afterburner. Reduce the throttle to 49 percent. Continue the climb.

Step 5. Level the aircraft at 20K. Use a slight amount of down elevator pitch.

Step 6. Using a Pilot Mode viewpoint, examine all of view directions.

Step 7. Bank 10 degrees left. Neutralize the bank. Continue the bank to a new heading of 0 degrees. When the new heading is reached level the aircraft.

Step 8. Pitch the aircraft's nose down. Use four keystrokes of the down elevator. Neutralize the pitch. Watch the Airspeed Indicator and the Frame Loading Indicator during this dive.

Step 9. Level the aircraft when an altitude of 1K is reached.

Step 10. Compensate for any loss in altitude with a slight amount of up elevator.

Altitude Change Test. Climb to an altitude of 20,000 feet. Reduce throttle to 49 percent and dive to an altitude of 5K. At the same throttle setting, climb back to an altitude of 10,000 feet.

You will receive a passing grade on this test if you can:

☐ Execute a climb.

☐ Execute a dive.

☐ Prevent aircraft stress and avoid stalls or a crash.

Alter Airspeed.

Step 1. Take off.

Step 2. Keep the afterburner engaged and retract the landing gear.

Step 3. Climb to an altitude of 500 feet and level the aircraft.

Step 4. Watch the indicated airspeed climb. At a speed of Mach 1.5, reduce the throttle to 49 percent.

Step 5. Climb to an altitude of 1K.

Step 6. Make a 45 degree bank to the left. At a new heading of 0 degrees, level the aircraft.

Step 7. Increase the throttle to 94 percent.

Step 8. Climb to an altitude of 20K. Level the aircraft at 20,000 feet.

Step 9. Reduce the throttle to 49 percent.

Step 10. Pitch the aircraft's nose down with 3 keystrokes. Neutralize the pitch.

Step 11. Observe the indicated airspeed.

Step 12. Level the aircraft at an altitude of 1K.

Step 13. Increase the throttle to 99 percent. Watch the rate of fuel consumption.

Step 14. After a loss of 4 percent of the fuel, engage the afterburner and watch the rate of fuel consumption.

Airspeed Test. At a fixed throttle of 49 percent, fluctuate the airspeed between Mach .5 and 1.0 without using the afterburner.

You will receive a passing grade on this test if you can:

☐ Control the aircraft's airspeed, altitude, and attitude through a fixed throttle control.

LESSON 3

Lesson Setup. If at any point during this lesson you crash the aircraft, just exit JET and return to the setup menus.

Select Aircraft Type.

Press 1 for F/A-18 practice.

Press 2 for F-16 practice.

Lesson Objectives. Learn three high-speed maneuvers (each maneuver is indicated in *italic* type) in the F/A-18 and the F-16.

Performing the Lesson. In order to have a reference "spot" on the forward canopy view, engage the Weapon Tracking Indicator.

High-Speed Maneuvers.

Step 1. Take off.

Step 2. Retract landing gear, but keep the afterburner engaged.

Step 3. Climb to an altitude of 20K.

Step 4. Level the aircraft at an altitude of 20K. Disengage the afterburner and reduce the throttle to 99 percent.

Step 5. *Bank* 45 degrees to the right. Neutralize the bank. Engage the afterburner.

Step 6. Keep the aircraft in this attitude and make several complete 360 degree circles.

Step 7. Level the aircraft and disengage the afterburner. Reduce the throttle to 84 percent.

Step 8. *Bank* 45 degrees to the left. Neutralize the bank. Keep throttle at 84 percent.

Step 9. Keep the aircraft in this attitude and make several complete 360 degree circles (Fig. 3-4). Notice the drop in the indicated airspeed. When the airspeed reaches Mach .1 to .2, the aircraft will start to lose altitude.

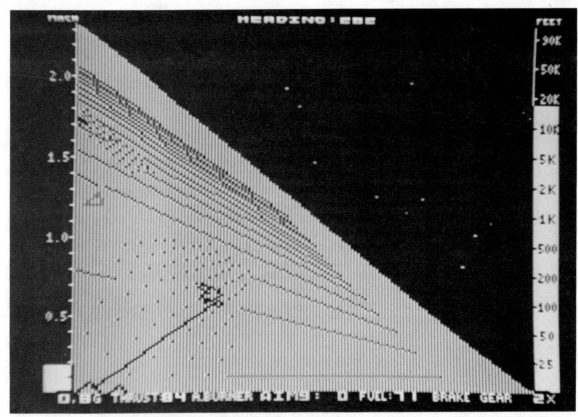

Fig. 3-4. Even though this high-performance bank has reduced the F-16's airspeed to a snail-like Mach .2, this is not slow enough to stall the aircraft. Understanding the stall threshold of your jet aircraft will be extremely helpful in the later missions.

Step 10. Level the aircraft.

Step 11. *Roll* right. Press and hold the right aileron key. Watch the Airspeed Indicator.

Step 12. After several revolutions, use the appropriate aileron keystroke to stop and level the aircraft. Compensate for any loss in altitude and climb back to an altitude of 20K.

Step 13. Increase the throttle to 99 percent. Engage the afterburner.

Step 14. *Loop* the aircraft. At an indicated airspeed of Mach 1, press and hold the up elevator key. The indicated airspeed will drop and the horizon will slowly appear along the top of the canopy. Continue to hold the up elevator. The aircraft will slowly pitch up until the true horizon once again appears. At this point, neutralize the pitch and level the aircraft.

High-speed Maneuvers Test. Climb to an altitude of 20K feet and do one roll, bank 360 degrees to the left, level the aircraft, do three rolls to the right, level the aircraft, bank 360 degrees to the right, level the aircraft, execute six rolls to the left, level the aircraft, and do two consecutive loops.

You will receive a passing grade on this test if you can:

☐ Do the correct number of iterations for each maneuver.
☐ Avoid any excessive loss in altitude.
☐ Perform all of the maneuvers without either stressing or crashing the aircraft.

LESSON 4

Lesson Setup. If at any point during this lesson you crash the aircraft, just exit JET and return to the setup menus.

Select Aircraft Type.

Press 1 for F/A-18 practice.

Press 2 for F-16 practice.

Lesson Objectives. Practice emergency flight procedures for the F/A-18 and the F-16. These are all potentially lifesaving lessons that will be used repeatedly in Part II's historical aviation scenarios.

Performing the Lesson. In order to have a reference ''spot'' on the forward canopy view, engage the Weapon Tracking Indicator.

Emergency Procedures.

Half-power takeoff.

Step 1. Assume a standard takeoff posture.

Step 2. Increase throttle to 54 percent and don't engage the afterburner.

Step 3. Follow a standard takeoff roll. (Press the L key with the F/A-18 version.)

0 percent throttle on landing.

Step 1. Line up for a standard landing.

Step 2. At an altitude of 1K feet, reduce the throttle to 0 percent.

Step 3. Avoid raising the nose of the aircraft for alignment with the far end of the runway or carrier.

Step 4. Follow a typical landing, but don't lower the landing gear or engage the speed brake until the aircraft is over the edge of the runway or carrier threshold.

Step 5. At the edge of the runway or carrier, lower the landing gear and engage the speed brake.

Step 6. Touch down. (Make sure that the F/A-18 engages the arresting cable.)

Stall.

Step 1. Climb to an altitude of 20K feet.

Step 2. Reduce the throttle to 49 percent.

Step 3. When the airspeed has dropped to Mach .7, try to loop the aircraft.

Step 4. The aircraft will stall. Immediately neutralize the pitch.

Step 5. Point the aircraft's nose towards the ground and level the aircraft (i.e., counteract any spinning, rolling, or rotation).

Step 6. As the indicated airspeed increases (above Mach .3), slowly give a slight amount of up elevator. Neutralize the pitch.

Step 7. Level the aircraft.

High-speed, low-altitude flight.

Step 1. Level the aircraft at an altitude of 500 feet.

Step 2. Engage the afterburner.

Step 3. Bank 45 degrees to the left. Neutralize the bank.

Step 4. After a bank of 360 degrees, level the aircraft.

Step 5. Reduce the aircraft's altitude to 200 feet and repeat the above bank.

Step 6. Reduce the aircraft's altitude to 100 feet and execute the same bank.

High-speed, small-radius turn.

Step 1. Climb to an altitude of 10K feet.

Step 2. Engage the afterburner.

Step 3. At an indicated airspeed of Mach 1.3, bank 90 degrees to the right. Neutralize the bank.

Step 4. In order to reduce the turning radius, slowly give a slight amount of up elevator. Neutralize the pitch.

Step 5. Watch the Airspeed Indicator, the Altimeter, and the Heading Indicator..

Step 6. Before the aircraft stalls, level the aircraft and neutralize all of the controls.

Ejection.

Step 1. Climb to an altitude of 5K feet.

Step 2. Reduce your airspeed to Mach .7.

Step 3. Pitch the nose of the aircraft down approximately 45 degrees.

Step 4. Eject from the jet fighter.

Step 5. Examine both viewpoints and all of the different view angles as you descend. Try various View Magnifications, also.

F-16-specific Emergency Procedures.

Half-runway takeoff.

Step 1. Taxi to the midpoint of runway 0.

Step 2. Apply full throttle and engage the afterburner.

Step 3. When the indicated airspeed reaches Mach .3, give a slight amount of up elevator.

Full-power landing.

Step 1. Assume a standard landing approach.

Step 2. Keep the throttle fixed at 99 percent. Don't engage the afterburner.

Step 3. Lower the landing gear and engage the speed brake.

Step 4. Avoid any excessive aircraft pitch.

Step 5. Fly the F-16 onto the runway. Immediately cut the throttle to 0 percent when the altimeter shows that you have landed.

Tarmac takeoff.

Step 1. Taxi out of the hangar.

Step 2. Turn to a heading of 180 degrees.

Step 3. Increase the throttle to 99 percent and engage the afterburner.

Step 4. When the indicated airspeed reaches Mach .3, give a slight amount of up elevator. Neutralize the pitch.

Step 5. Follow the rest of the standard F-16 takeoff procedure.

F/A-18-specific Emergency Procedures.

Full-power landing.

Step 1. Assume a standard landing approach.

Step 2. Keep the throttle fixed at 99 percent. Don't engage the afterburner.

Step 3. Lower the landing gear and engage the speed brake.

Step 4. Avoid any excessive aircraft pitch.

Step 5. Fly the F/A-18 directly onto the carrier's landing deck. Don't reduce the throttle. The arresting cable will ''catch'' the aircraft. If you bolter or miss the cable, retract the landing gear and disengage the speed brake. Slowly climb back to an altitude of 1K feet and circle for another landing attempt.

Note: This landing procedure exactly mimics that used by actual carrier-based aircraft.

Land from the other direction.

Step 1. Instead of landing from the west, land from the east.

Step 2. Approach the aircraft carrier from three miles east.

Step 3. Assume a heading of 270 degrees.

Step 4. Line up with the landing deck of the carrier. Use a higher View Magnification to check your aircraft's alignment.

Step 5. Reduce the throttle to 19 percent. Lower the landing gear and engage the speed brake.

Step 6. Land the aircraft on the bow of the carrier and continue your landing roll towards the carrier's stern.

Step 7. Engage the arresting cable.

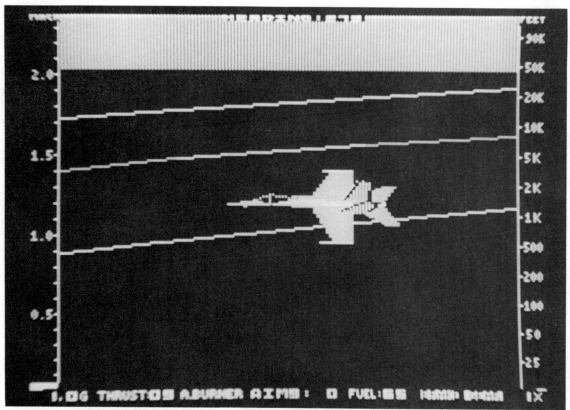

Fig. 3-5. Even if you miss the arresting cable, you can still taxi around on the carrier deck for attempting another pass. The speed brake must be engaged during all carrier deck travel.

Taxi on the carrier's deck.

Step 1. Make a standard landing approach.

Step 2. Gauge your point of contact with the carrier's deck slightly fore of the arresting cable.

Step 3. Lower the landing gear and engage the speed brake.

Step 4. Immediately reduce throttle to 4 percent when the aircraft lands on the carrier.

Step 5. With the speed brake still engaged, slowly turn the aircraft back towards the stern of the carrier. (*Note:* Failure to keep the speed brake engaged and the indicated airspeed low can cause the aircraft to skid off of the carrier's deck and crash.)

Step 6. Use the Control Tower Mode for watching the F/A-18 taxi about the carrier's deck (Fig. 3-5).

Step 7. Direct the aircraft towards the dotted line which represents the arresting cable.

Step 8. Contact with the cable will complete the landing.

Emergency Procedure Test. Successfully perform all of these emergency procedures by using different test criteria. For example, try different altitudes, attitudes, and airspeeds during each emergency procedure.

You will receive a passing grade on this test if you can:

☐ Understand the physical properties behind the operation of each emergency procedure.

☐ Perform any procedure under a wide variety of different conditions.

☐ Execute each procedure without suffering any aircraft damage or pilot loss.

Chapter 4

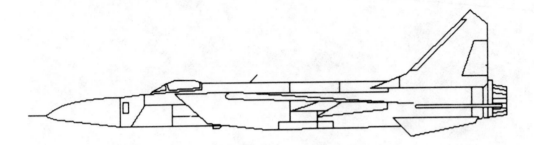

Solo Flight

Now that you have completed both your basic and advanced jet fighter flight instruction, it is time to test your competence in handling your aircraft. The following two tests will push your physical and mental abilities to their limits. If you are able to successfully complete both of these flight tests, then you can consider yourself to have graduated with honors from the JET flight school. Make sure that you have passed these tests and earned your wings before you attempt any of the historical aviation scenarios that are contained in Part II. It is far better to evaluate your level of jet flying proficiency at this time than later, when three MiGs are studying your six.

F-16 Flight Test Setup. If you should crash your aircraft during this test, just exit JET and return to the startup menus.

Select Game Mode.
Press 3.
Choose Skill Level.
Press 5.
Select Aircraft Type.
Press 2.
Test Objectives. Test the jet handling proficiency of the JET pilot.
Taking the Test.
Step 1. Take off from runway 4L.
Step 2. Climb to an altitude of 30,000 feet with an indicated airspeed of Mach .9.
Step 3. Accelerate to an indicated airspeed of Mach 1.5.
Step 4. Climb to an altitude of 40,000 feet and accelerate to Mach 2.
Step 5. Assume a new heading of 313 degrees and reduce airspeed to Mach 1.
Step 6. Climb to an altitude of 50,000 feet. Turn to a heading of 215 degrees.
Step 7. Reduce your altitude to 20,000 feet.
Step 8. Reduce throttle to 0 percent.
Step 9. Activate the Attitude Indicator. Pitch the aircraft's nose up 90 degrees.
Step 10. Deactivate the Attitude Indicator.

Step 11. Recover from the stall at an altitude of 10,000 feet.

Step 12. Turn to a new heading of 180 degrees.

Step 13. Restart the jet engine and increase the throttle.

Step 14. Make a landing approach on runway 0.

Step 15. Perform a touch-and-go landing on runway 0.

Step 16. Climb to an altitude of 1,000 feet.

Step 17. Make a 90 degree bank to the right on a new heading of 100 degrees.

Step 18. Cross the home airbase at an altitude of 500 feet with a heading of 270 degrees.

Step 19. Execute three left rolls over the airbase's control tower.

Step 20. Land on runway 22L and park in the hangar.

Test Debriefing. You will receive a passing grade on this test if you:

☐ Performed each maneuver perfectly.

☐ Didn't overtax either the airframe or the pilot. In other words, the Frame Loading Indicator stayed within the −3 to 9G tolerance zone.

☐ Landed the F-16 with at least 70 percent of its fuel remaining.

F/A-18 Flight Test Setup. If you should crash your aircraft during this test, just exit JET and return to the startup menus.

Select Game Mode.

Press 3.

Choose Skill Level.

Press 5.

Select Aircraft Type.

Press 1.

Test Objectives. Test the jet handling proficiency of the JET pilot.

Taking the Test.

Step 1. Take off from the carrier with 49 percent thrust.

Step 2. Climb to an altitude of 30,000 feet and accelerate to an indicated airspeed of Mach .9.

Step 3. Accelerate to an indicated airspeed of Mach 1.5.

Step 4. Climb to an altitude of 40,000 feet and accelerate to Mach 2.

Step 5. Assume a new heading of 350 degrees and reduce airspeed to Mach 1.

Step 6. Climb to an altitude of 50,000 feet. Turn to a heading of 265 degrees.

Step 7. Reduce your altitude to 20,000 feet.

Step 8. Reduce throttle to 0 percent.

Step 9. Activate the Attitude Indicator. Pitch the aircraft's nose up 90 degrees.

Step 10. Deactivate the Attitude Indicator.

Step 11. Recover from the stall at an altitude of 10,000 feet.

Step 12. Turn to a new heading of 260 degrees.

Step 13. Restart the jet engine and increase the throttle.

Step 14. Make a landing approach on the bow of the carrier.

Step 15. Perform a touch-and-go landing fore of the arresting cable (i.e., bolter the cable).

Step 16. Climb to an altitude of 1,000 feet.

Step 17. Make a 90 degree bank to the left on a new heading of 180 degrees.

Step 18. Fly over the carrier from starboard to port with the F/A-18 in inverted flight at an altitude of 500 feet on a heading of 0 degrees.

Step 19. Turn to a heading of 220 degrees and return to a normal flight attitude.

Step 20. Land on the carrier and engage the arresting cable.

Test Results. You will receive a passing grade on this test if you:

☐ Performed each maneuver perfectly.

Certificate of JET Solo Flight

This is to acknowledge that,

did professionally and competently
pass the rigorous JET solo flight
course on

Possession of this certificate grants
the bearer the right to fly an advanced
jet aircraft in any historical aviation
scenario.

Fig. 4-1. After you have successfully completed the solo flight test, place your name and the day's date on this certificate.

☐ Didn't overtax either the airframe or the pilot. In other words, the Frame Loading Indicator stayed within the −3 to 9G tolerance zone.
☐ Landed the F/A-18 with at least 50 percent of its fuel remaining.

Once you have passed both of these tests, your flying competence in a modern jet fighter

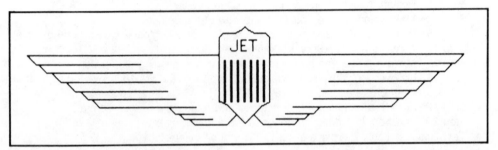

Fig. 4-2. As an acknowledgment of your soloing, cut these wings from this book and pin them to the front of your shirt. Wear them proudly.

is beyond reproach. Interestingly enough, much of the material from both of these tests is exactly duplicated from the actual F-16 and F/A-18 pilot testing program. Therefore, your flight simulation skill is steeped in genuine performance criteria.

Only two final duties await your attention before proceeding to the air combat missions contained in Part II. First, the Flight Graduation Citation in Fig. 4-1 should be completed with your name. After all, you earned it. Second, lacking a full-scale ceremony, make a copy of the wings insignia in Fig. 4-2. Then, pin this most prestigious of pilot awards to the front of your flight suit. Wear them proudly as you fly the following historical aviation scenarios.

Part 2
JET Missions

A marvelous attribute of *JET* is its ability to recreate virtually any historical jet aircraft activity from the relatively recent annals of jet aviation history. Almost any event can be thoroughly and realistically represented through the manipulation of the F-16 and F/A-18 silhouettes and their associated menu parameters. Throw in a modest amount of imagination and you will soon be flying Israeli Mirages against fortified Sinai SAM positions or landing British Sea Harrier jets on the rocking deck of the carrier *HMS Invincible*.

In the following 82 scenarios, the most exciting and memorable jet aircraft activities from 1944 to the present day are carefully recreated for use with *JET*. Each chapter depicts a single historical event that has been fully documented to ensure its adherence to fact. In other words, throttle settings, altimeter readings, selected armaments, and indicated airspeeds have all been painstakingly monitored for an exact duplication of the performance specifications that are represented by the aircraft from each particular scenario. Additionally, if the pilot of the actual historical aircraft scored a successful mission, then you too will be expected to match this feat. All in all, you will witness the thrill of flying in a real-life situation without suffering the discomfort of losing your life.

The format used in each of these historical scenarios is similar to the structure that was used in the preceding instructional chapters. Following a brief historical introduction to the events surrounding the scenario, the **Mission Setup** steps through the required responses for each of the *JET* menus. Then, with your aircraft ready to go, the **Mission Objectives** are outlined. These are the goals that should be met for successfully completing the scenario. Next, **Flying the Mission** gives a short step-by-step accounting of the procedure that should be used for achieving the mission objectives. Finally, the **Mission Debriefing** grades your performance in meeting the mission objectives.

Most of the action contained within a scenario involves either aerial or air-to-ground combat. In these cases, a successfully fulfilled mission will require the downing of enemy aircraft or the destruction of specified ground targets. There are two means for determining whether or not these criteria have been accomplished. First, a rising tone will be heard through the computer's speaker when an enemy aircraft or target has been destroyed. Second, a black "kill" mark will appear on the rearward side of your aircraft's left fuselage panel as a registration of your victory. If you fail to hear the tone, you can use a Backward View with a View Magnification of 1 × to see if your kill has been correctly recorded.

Just as you will be firing at the enemy, they will be most assuredly shooting back at you. Basically, this enemy fire can be detected by four methods. First, if the Radar System Display is active, all of the enemy missiles will appear as moving white dots. This is your best method for monitoring the course of the combat around your aircraft. The second way to determine the presence of hostile fire is to receive a visual sighting. Once again, missiles will appear as moving white dots from any view direction. Another indicator of the proximity of dangerous fire is a warning tone, which beeps when a missile is within several hundred yards of your aircraft. Usually, by the time you hear this sound, it is too late. Your last method for determining the location of enemy missiles is actually the worst of all. When a missile hits your aircraft, the screen will flash several times and the aircraft will pitch and roll violently. At this point, you have only one recourse— eject. Therefore, if at all possible, try to rely on the first two forms of missile avoidance, because the final two methods can be extremely painful.

Of course, there will be times when a missile that is tracking you requires an immediate form of evasive action. At this crucial moment, your first thought will be to try and outrun the missile. *Forget it*. Turning on an afterburner only serves as a strong attraction for the guidance system of the missile. You would be far smarter to refrain from using the afterburner and try for altitude and attitude differences, instead. If your aircraft is higher than the missile, it will consume its fuel faster trying to reach you (in return, your missiles will have an advantage when fired from this higher altitude). Also, holding a tight spiraling turn will force the missile to duplicate this maneuver and exhaust its fuel quicker. Just remember that each missile has a limited range, and once you have shaken the enemy's fire it will be your turn to do some shooting.

Each scenario is self-contained; only the *JET* software is necessary for satisfying the mission objectives. For the most part, subLOGIC Scenery Disks shouldn't be used with these scenarios. The use of a Scenery Disk eliminates the ability for *JET* to be used in anything other than its free flight mode. Furthermore, even the free flight mode experiences a slight aberration when these disks are used. The Fuel Quantity Indicator remains fixed at 99 percent. Granted, this condition is great for unlimited flying, but any degree of realism is lost.

On the other hand, Missions 51 and 52 could make use of a Scenery Disk. These two chapters duplicate the aerobatic performance of the U.S. Air Force Thunderbirds and US Navy Blue Angels, respectively. By using a Scenery Disk, these aerobatic teams could give their demonstrations in a more realistic setting. Your Thunderbird F-16 and Blue Angel A-4, however, will still be hampered by a faulty fuel indicator. Therefore, for the highest degree of realism, avoid the use of Scenery Disks.

Chapter 5

World War II

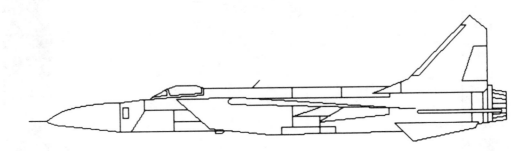

1. THE BIRTH OF THE JET

On 27 August 1939, an odd aircraft took to the air over prewar Germany. The Heinkel He 178 was a single-engined aircraft that used the new concept of turbojet power as its means of propulsion. Several years later, Willy Messerschmitt and his Bayerische Flugzeugwerke AG (later the Messerschmitt AG) had produced the first operational jet fighter in quantity. The Me 262A-1a *Schwalbe* (Swallow) jet fighter saw its first concerted action in the JG7 fighter unit based at Achmer and Hesepe, Germany, on 3 October 1944 under the command of Major Walter Nowotny.

Mission Setup.

Select Game Mode.

Press 1.

Choose Skill Level.

Press 0.

Select Aircraft Type.

Press 2.

Select Armament.

Press 1 three times. Total 0.

Press 2 three times. Total 0.

Press 5.

Your Me 262A-1a has a top speed of Mach .7 at a maximum altitude of 36,000 feet.

Do not use the Radar System Display, the Weapon Tracking Indicator, or the Attitude Indicator. The afterburner may not be used during this scenario.

Your only armament is four 30mm MK108 cannons in your jet's nose.

Mission Objectives. Score the first jet fighter aerial kill.

Flying the Mission.

Step 1. Use a tarmac takeoff technique.

Step 2. Never exceed an indicated airspeed of Mach .7 or an altitude of 36,000 feet.

Step 3. Activate the M61A1 Weapon System. Fire off 400 rounds of your 500 rounds of ammunition. You now have a total of 100 rounds of cannon ammunition for combat.

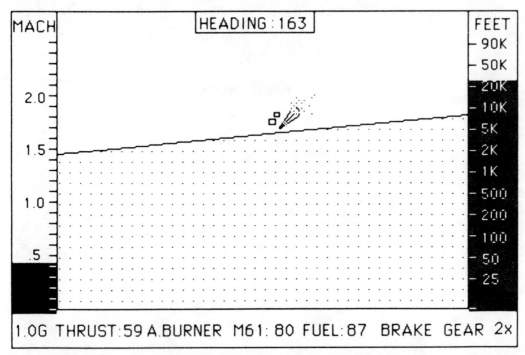

HEADING : 163

FEET

90K

50K

2.0

20K

10K

1.5

5K

2K

1K

1.0

500

200

100

.5

50

25

1.0G THRUST:59 A.BURNER M61:80 FUEL:87 BRAKE GEAR 2x

Fig. 5-1. Using only 20 rounds of ammunition, this Me 262A-1a has shot down an allied bomber somewhere over Germany.

Step 4. Intercept and shoot down the enemy aircraft (Fig. 5-1).

Step 5. Return to base and land.

Step 6. Immediately taxi into the hangar.

Mission Debriefing. You will have successfully flown this mission if you:

☐ Stayed within the performance boundaries of the Me 262A-1a.

☐ Shot down at least one enemy aircraft with a maximum of 100 rounds of ammunition.

☐ Safely completed the mission.

2. THE FIRST JET FIGHTER/BOMBER

The Me 262 aircraft was a bird of two feathers. In addition to being used as a splendid fighter (Me 262A-1a), a fighter/bomber version was also developed, the Me 262A-2a *Sturmvogel*. The success of the Me 262A-2a was far less glamorous than its fighter cousin. Following several limited and unproductive actions, the largest Me 262A-2a fighter/bomber unit, IV/KG 51 based at Achmer, Germany, was grounded in 1945 with all of its aircraft either destroyed during Allied bombing attacks or captured by the advancing Allied armies.

    Mission Setup.

    Select Game Mode.

    Press 2.

Choose Skill Level.
Press 0.
Select Aircraft Type.
Press 2.
Select Armament.
Press 3 three times. Total 0.
Press 4 five times. Total 2.
Press 5.
Your Me 262A-2a has a top speed of Mach .7 at a maximum altitude of 36,000 feet.
Do not use the Radar System Display, the Weapon Tracking Indicator, or the Attitude Indicator.
The afterburner may not be used during this scenario.
Your armament is four 30mm MK108 cannons in your jet's nose and two 500kg bombs.
Mission Objectives. Make a successful jet fighter/bomber attack.
Flying the Mission.
Step 1. Use a tarmac takeoff technique.
Step 2. Never exceed an indicated airspeed of Mach .7 or an altitude of 36,000 feet.
Step 3. Activate the M61A1 Weapon System. Fire off 400 rounds of your 500 rounds of ammunition. You now have a total of 100 rounds of cannon ammunition for combat.
Step 4. Bomb the selected target that is located near the France/Germany border. Also, use your 100 rounds of cannon fire in strafing runs over the target.
Step 5. Return to base and land.
Step 6. Immediately taxi into the hangar.
Mission Debriefing. You will have successfully flown this mission if you:

☐ Stayed within the performance boundaries of the Me 262A-2a.
☐ Successfully bombed and strafed the enemy target. (This is an interesting point: In reality, very few of the "real" Me 262A-2a bombing missions were ever successful.)
☐ Safely completed the mission.

3. ROCKET FLEA

As the Allied air war effort stripped Germany of its vital petroleum reservoirs, alternate methods of power were devised. Accompanying these radical power supplies were special aircraft that could fly with these unconventional fuels. Dr. Alexander Lippisch designed an operational fighter, the Me 163B-1a Komet, that used a rocket motor as its propulsion source. Two hypergolic fuels, *T-Stoff* (hydrogen peroxide and oxyquinoline) and *C-Stoff* (hydrazine hydrate, methanol, and water) served as the power source for the aircraft's rocket motor. The sensitive nature of this fuel source actually destroyed more Me 163s than were shot down by Allied fighters. Only one true unit of these rocket fighters was organized: I/JG 400 at Brandis, Germany, was formed in 1944 and flew its first interception flight on 16 August 1944.
Mission Setup.
Select Game Mode.
Press 1.
Choose Skill Level.
Press 0.
Select Aircraft Type.

Press 2.

Select Armament.

Press 1 three times. Total 0.

Press 2 three times. Total 0.

Press 5.

Your Me 163B-1a has a top speed of Mach .8 at a maximum altitude of 39,000 feet.

Only 10 percent of the rocket fighter's fuel may be used before the throttle must be reduced to 0 percent.

All landings must be performed with a throttle setting of 0 percent.

Do not use the Radar System Display, the Weapon Tracking Indicator, or the Attitude Indicator. The afterburner may not be used during this scenario.

Your only armament is two 30mm MK108 cannons in your aircraft's wing roots.

Mission Objectives. Score the first rocket fighter aerial kill.

Flying the Mission.

Step 1. Use a tarmac takeoff technique.

Step 2. Never exceed an indicated airspeed of Mach .8. Try to maintain a steep 45 degree pitch climb.

Step 3. Climb to an altitude of 20,000 feet. Don't climb higher than an altitude of 36,000 feet. Level off at 25,000 feet.

Step 4. Activate the M61A1 Weapon System. Fire off 440 rounds of your 500 rounds of ammunition. You now have a total of 60 rounds of cannon ammunition for combat.

Step 5. Intercept and shoot down the enemy aircraft. When your Fuel Quantity Indicator reads 89 percent, decrease the throttle to 0 percent.

Step 6. Use the remainder of your fuel, if you have any left above the 89 percent limit, to return to base.

Step 7. Make a 0 percent throttle landing at the base.

Mission Debriefing. You will have successfully flown this mission if you:

☐ Stayed within the performance boundaries of the Me 163B-1a.
☐ Shot down at least one enemy aircraft with a maximum of 60 rounds of ammunition.
☐ Used only 10 percent of your fuel.
☐ Safely completed the mission.

4. A STRATEGIC JET BOMBER

Operation *Bodenplatte* was one final, grand Luftwaffe attempt at crushing the backbone of the dominant Allied air forces. On 1 January 1945, approximately 800 German fighters and fighter/bombers attacked Allied air bases throughout western Europe. The plan caught the Allies napping and 500 British and American aircraft were destroyed on the ground at the cost of 300 German aircraft (many of which were shot down by careless German antiaircraft gunners). The most noteworthy German aircraft to take part in this raid was the first dedicated jet bomber, the Arado Ar 234B-2 Blitz. Carrying two 1000kg bombs, the Ar 234B-2 combined the speed and and operational altitude of a contemporary piston-powered fighter with the payload of a light bomb-er. The age of the strategic bomber had been born.

Mission Setup.

Select Game Mode.
Press 2.
Choose Skill Level.
Press 0.
Select Aircraft Type.
Press 2.
Select Armament.
Press 3 three times. Total 0.
Press 4 five times. Total 2.
Press 5.
Your Ar 234B-2 has a top speed of Mach .6 at a maximum altitude of 40,000 feet.
Do not use the Radar System Display, the Weapon Tracking Indicator, or the Attitude Indicator.
The afterburner may not be used during this scenario.
Your armament is two 1000kg bombs.
Mission Objectives. Successfully bomb the western Europe Allied target.
Flying the Mission.
Step 1. Take off from runway 18.
Step 2. Never exceed an indicated airspeed of Mach .6 or an altitude of 10,000 feet. You will be approaching the target low and fast.
Step 3. The Ar 234B-2 lacks any cannon armament. Therefore, don't use your M61A1 cannon on the bombing runs. You will only use the two 1000kg bombs during this mission.
Step 4. Bomb the selected target, which is located near Brussels.
Step 5. Return to base and land.
Step 6. Immediately taxi into the hangar.
Mission Debriefing. You will have successfully flown this mission if you:

☐ Stayed within the performance boundaries of the AR 234B-2.
☐ Successfully bombed the enemy target. (In the actual Operation *Bodenplatte,* there are no records of damage being inflicted by bomb-laden Ar 234B-2s.)
☐ Safely completed the mission.

5. KAMIKAZE

With the tide of the Pacific War turning against Japan, a new aerial warfare plan was initiated. *Kamikaze* or *shimpu* (Divine Wind) attacks were flown against all American capital ships within striking distance of these newly created Special Attack Units. Flying outdated aircraft that had been packed with explosives, these suicide flights imparted varying degrees of damage to the American naval fleets. In an effort to give the *shimpu* pilot an advantage in reaching his naval goal, Ensign Ohta designed a rocket-powered suicide aircraft. The Yokosuka MXY-7 Ohka (Cherry Blossom) was carried in the bomb bay of a Mitsubishi G4M1 Betty and released 3 to 10 miles away from the naval target. The Ohka pilot, armed with 1200kg of explosives, would then fly his aircraft into the nearest American capital ship. Hopefully—for the Japanese, that is—the resultant explosion would sink the vessel.
    Mission Setup.
    Select Game Mode.

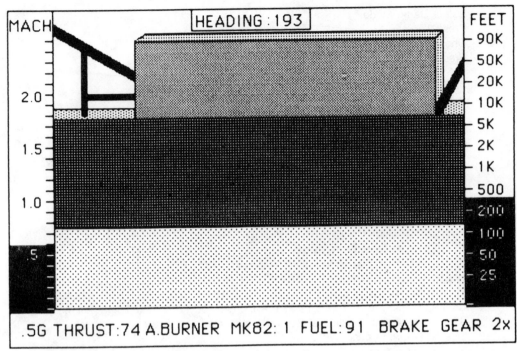

Fig. 5-2. The final view for a kamikaze pilot. The 1200kg bomb payload should be released at this point.

Press 2.
Choose Skill Level.
Press 0.
Select Aircraft Type.
Press 1.
Select Armament.
Press 3 three times. Total 0.
Press 4 four times. Total 1.
Press 5.
Your MXY-7 has a top speed of Mach .7 at a maximum altitude of 18,000 feet.
Do not use the Radar System Display, the Weapon Tracking Indicator, or the Attitude Indicator.
The afterburners may not be used during this scenario.
Your armament is one 1200kg explosive payload.
Mission Objectives. Sink an American capital ship in a suicide crash.
Flying the Mission.
Step 1. Take off from the aircraft carrier.
Step 2. Assume an altitude of 18,000 feet.
Step 3. Line up with the target vessel. Never exceed an indicated airspeed of Mach .7. You will use a steep glide path into the ship.
Step 4. The MXY-7 lacks any cannon armament. Therefore, don't use your M61A1 cannon on the bombing runs. You will only use the one 1200kg payload during this mission.
Step 5. Ram your aircraft into the hull of the target ship (Fig. 5-2). Just before the collision, release your single 1200kg payload.
Mission Debriefing. You will have successfully flown this mission if you:

☐ Stayed within the performance boundaries of the MXY-7.
☐ Successfully crashed into the enemy target. A total of 74 Ohka missions were flown by the Japanese. Only four of these rocket-powered bombs ever reached their targets (most were destroyed while still in the bomb bays of the G4M1s). All four, however, did score hits on the American vessels.
☐ *Failed* to return from the mission.

Chapter 6

Korean War

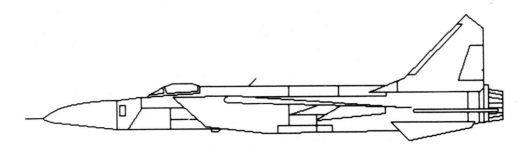

6. 8 NOVEMBER 1950

With the outbreak of the Korean War, American air power was once again flying over foreign soil. These missions, however, were vastly different from those flown over Europe and the Pacific. Aerial warfare had changed dramatically since the introduction of jet fighters in the latter years of World War II. The U.S. Air Force had to create new aircraft designs that could compete with the performance capabilities of foreign jets. An initial attempt at an American jet fighter was the Lockheed P-80 Shooting Star (later renamed the F-80). As the Communist threat began to increase in Korea, small numbers of F-80C jet fighters began to appear. A historic footnote to this aircraft introduction was logged on 8 November 1950 by Lt. Russell J. Brown. Flying an F-80C, Lt. Brown shot down an enemy MiG jet in the world's first jet vs. jet aerial duel.

Mission Setup.
Select Game Mode.
Press 1.
Choose Skill Level.
Press 0.
Select Aircraft Type.
Press 2.
Select Armament.
Press 1 three times. Total 0.
Press 2 three times. Total 0.
Press 5.
Your F-80C has a top speed of Mach .7 at a maximum altitude of 42,000 feet.
Do not use the Radar System Display, the Weapon Tracking Indicator, or the Attitude Indicator.
The afterburner may not be used during this scenario. Your only armament is six .50-caliber M3 machine guns in your jet's nose.
Mission Objectives. Score the first jet vs. jet aerial kill.

Flying the Mission.

Step 1. Take off from runway 22L.

Step 2. Never exceed an indicated airspeed of Mach .7 or an altitude of 42,000 feet.

Step 3. Activate the M61A1 Weapon System. Fire off 300 rounds of your 500 rounds of ammunition. You now have a total of 200 rounds of machine gun ammunition for combat.

Step 4. Intercept and shoot down the enemy aircraft.

Step 5. Return to base and land.

Step 6. Taxi into the hangar.

Mission Debriefing. You will have successfully flown this mission if you:

☐ Stayed within the performance boundaries of the F-80C.

☐ Shot down at least one enemy aircraft with a maximum of 200 rounds of ammunition.

☐ Safely completed the mission.

7. 17 DECEMBER 1950

The introduction of the Communist MiG-15 quickly put the U.S. Air Force at an aerial combat inferiority. Gone were the days of American dominance of the skies over Korea. Even the Lockheed F-80C was at a minor disadvantage in engagements with the MiG-15. In response to this crisis, the North American F-86A Sabre was shipped into the Korean combat zone. After several sorties, the first F-86A and MiG-15 encounter occurred. Lt. Colonel Bruce H. Hinton claimed the first MiG-15 kill by an F-86A pilot. In the years that followed, the F-86 would become the world's best MiG-killer.

Mission Setup.

Select Game Mode.

Press 1.

Choose Skill Level.

Press 0.

Select Aircraft Type.

Press 2.

Select Armament.

Press 1 three times. Total 0.

Press 2 three times. Total 0.

Press 5.

Your F-86A has a top speed of Mach .9 at a maximum altitude of 50,000 feet.

Do not use the Radar System Display, the Weapon Tracking Indicator, or the Attitude Indicator. The afterburner may not be used during this scenario.

Your only armament is six .50-caliber M3 machine guns in your jet's nose.

Mission Objectives. Score the first F-86A kill.

Flying the Mission.

Step 1. Take off from runway 22L.

Step 2. Never exceed an indicated airspeed of Mach .9 or an altitude of 50,000 feet.

Step 3. Activate the M61A1 Weapon System. Fire off 300 rounds of your 500 rounds of ammunition. You now have a total of 200 rounds of machine gun ammunition for combat.

Step 4. Intercept and shoot down the enemy aircraft.

Step 5. Return to base and perform a victory roll over the base.

Step 6. Land and taxi into the hangar.

Mission Debriefing. You will have successfully flown this mission if you:

☐ Stayed within the performance boundaries of the F-86A.

☐ Shot down at least one enemy aircraft with a maximum of 200 rounds of ammunition.

☐ Safely completed the mission.

8. BIG DAY

Once the F-86A had drawn MiG-15 blood, the Sabre pilots began to sweep the enemy jets from the Korean sky. Several minor engagements filled the days of December 1950. Finally, the first major jet aircraft aerial battle broke out on 22 December 1950. Eight F-86As tangled with 15 MiG-15s near the Yalu river. The result was that six MiG-15s were shot down with no losses to the American Sabre jets.

Mission Setup.

Select Game Mode.

Press 1.

Choose Skill Level.

Press 0.

Select Aircraft Type.

Press 2.

Select Armament.

Press 1 three times. Total 0.

Press 2 three times. Total 0.

Press 5.

Your F-86A has a top speed of Mach .9 at a maximum altitude of 50,000 feet.

Do not use the Radar System Display, the Weapon Tracking Indicator, or the Attitude Indicator. The afterburner may not be used during this scenario.

Your only armament is six .50-caliber M3 machine guns in your jet's nose.

Mission Objectives. Score six MiG-15 kills.

Flying the Mission.

Step 1. Take off from runway 22L.

Step 2. Never exceed an indicated airspeed of Mach .9 or an altitude of 50,000 feet.

Step 3. Activate the M61A1 Weapon System. Fire off 300 rounds of your 500 rounds of ammunition. You now have a total of 200 rounds of machine gun ammunition for combat.

Step 4. Intercept and shoot down six enemy aircraft. This effort will require staying aloft for a lengthy patrol time. Judicious use of the throttle will help to conserve fuel during this mission.

Step 5. Return to base and perform six victory rolls over the base.

Step 6. Land and taxi into the hangar.

Mission Debriefing. You will have successfully flown this mission if you:

☐ Stayed within the performance boundaries of the F-86A.

- ☐ Shot down all six of the enemy aircraft with a maximum of 200 rounds of ammunition.
- ☐ Safely completed the mission.

9. 100 MiG-15s

Slowly the Communist pilots learned how to exploit the virtues of their MiG-15s over the highly skilled Sabre pilots. This slight swing in the quest for air superiority over Korea brought revisions to the F-86A airframe. The next major design improvement was the F-86E. The greatest structural improvement found in the F-86E was the use of a moving horizontal stabilizer, or "all-flying tail." This feature made the entire stabilizer act as an elevator for controlling the pitch of the aircraft. The result was a more maneuverable Sabre. Actually, the F-86E arrived none too early as 34 F-86Es and 55 F-84Es were jumped by 100 MiG-15s near Namsi. After the dust had cleared, six MiGs had been destroyed and one F-84E had been shot down.

Mission Setup.
Select Game Mode.
Press 1.
Choose Skill Level.
Press 0.
Select Aircraft Type.
Press 2.
Select Armament.
Press 1 three times. Total 0.
Press 2 three times. Total 0.
Press 5.
Your F-86E has a top speed of Mach .9 at a maximum altitude of 50,000 feet.
Do not use the Radar System Display, the Weapon Tracking Indicator, or the Attitude Indicator. The afterburner may not be used during this scenario.
Your only armament is six .50-caliber M3 machine guns in your jet's nose.
Mission Objectives. Score six MiG-15 kills.
Flying the Mission.
Step 1. Take off from runway 22L.
Step 2. Never exceed an indicated airspeed of Mach .9 or an altitude of 50,000 feet.
Step 3. Activate the M61A1 Weapon System. Fire off 300 rounds of your 500 rounds of ammunition. You now have a total of 200 rounds of machine gun ammunition for combat.
Step 4. Intercept and shoot down six enemy aircraft. In order to bag your MiG limit, you may need to remain on patrol for an extended period of time. Judicious use of the throttle will help to conserve fuel during this mission.
Step 5. Return to base and land.
Step 6. Taxi into the hangar.
Mission Debriefing. You will have successfully flown this mission if you:

- ☐ Stayed within the performance boundaries of the F-86E.
- ☐ Shot down all six of the enemy aircraft with a maximum of 200 rounds of ammunition.
- ☐ Safely completed the mission.

10. McCONNELL'S MiGs

The complete domination of an American fighter over foreign soil has never been as total as that exhibited by the Sabre jets in the Korean War (in fact, many pilots from the Vietnam War longed for even a glimmer of this former supremacy). Looking at the records logged by Korean-era jet fighters highlights two remarkable points. First, there were a total of 39 Allied aces during the war. And second, all 39 of these aces flew an F-86 aircraft. Studying the achievements of the F-86 in greater depth shows that the Sabre pilot enjoyed an astonishing 14-to-1 kills-versus-losses ratio. The leader of this flock of F-86 aces was a pilot with the 51st Fighter/Interceptor Wing—Joseph McConnell. McConnell finished the war with 16 MiG-15 kills.

Mission Setup.
Select Game Mode.
Press 1.
Choose Skill Level.
Press 0.
Select Aircraft Type.
Press 2.
Select Armament.
Press 1 three times. Total 0.
Press 2 three times. Total 0.
Press 5.
Your F-86F has a top speed of Mach .9 at a maximum altitude of 50,000 feet.
Do not use the Radar System Display, the Weapon Tracking Indicator, or the Attitude Indicator. The afterburner may not be used during this scenario.
Your only armament is six .50-caliber M3 machine guns in your jet's nose.
Mission Objectives. Score 16 MiG-15 kills.
Flying the Mission.
Step 1. Take off from runway 22L.
Step 2. Never exceed an indicated airspeed of Mach .9 or an altitude of 50,000 feet.
Step 3. Activate the M61A1 Weapon System. Fire off 300 rounds of your 500 rounds of ammunition. You now have a total of 200 rounds of machine gun ammunition for combat.
Step 4. Intercept and shoot down 16 enemy aircraft. Because McConnell scored his impressive victory total over several missions, you may return to base and refuel and rearm as many times as are needed to complete this scenario. You will need to taxi into the hangar to complete your fueling and armament selection. Be sure to heed Steps 1, 2, and 3 following each landing.
Step 5. Return to base and land.
Step 6. Taxi into the hangar.
Mission Debriefing. You will have successfully flown this mission if you:

☐ Stayed within the performance boundaries of the F-86F.
☐ Shot down all 16 enemy aircraft.
☐ Safely completed the mission.

11. NAVAL FIGHTERS

Just as U.S. Navy fighters had scoured the air throughout the Pacific some five years earlier, U.S. Navy jets now filled the skies over Korea. Leading the way for the Navy's aerial contribution to the Korean War was the Grumman F9F-2 Panther. This sleek jet fighter was launched from and recovered on conventional aircraft carriers. A single Pratt & Whitney engine provided the Panther with its power. Naval Panther jet operations had been under way for five months before the first MiG-15 was encountered. An F9F-2 of VF-111 claimed the first jet kill for a U.S. Navy jet fighter.

Mission Setup.
Select Game Mode.
Press 1.
Choose Skill Level.
Press 0.
Select Aircraft Type.
Press 1.
Select Armament.
Press 1 three times. Total 0.
Press 2 three times. Total 0.
Press 5.
Your F9F-2 has a top speed of Mach .7 at a maximum altitude of 42,000 feet.
Do not use the Radar System Display, the Weapon Tracking Indicator, or the Attitude Indicator.
The afterburner may not be used during this scenario.
Your only armament is four 20mm cannons in your jet's nose.
Mission Objectives. Shoot down one MiG-15.
Flying the Mission.
Step 1. Take off from the aircraft carrier.
Step 2. Never exceed an indicated airspeed of Mach .7 or an altitude of 42,000 feet.
Step 3. Activate the M61A1 Weapon System. Fire off 300 rounds of your 500 rounds of ammunition. You now have a total of 200 rounds of machine gun ammunition for combat.
Step 4. Intercept and shoot down the enemy aircraft.
Step 5. Return to the aircraft carrier and land.
Mission Debriefing. You will have successfully flown this mission if you:

☐ Stayed within the performance boundaries of the F9F-2.
☐ Shot down one enemy aircraft with a maximum of 200 rounds of ammunition.
☐ Safely completed the mission.

12. HWACHON DAM

As the war extended into its second year, the bulk of the U.S. naval aircraft were relegated to ground strike roles. Prominent among these aircraft were the Navy's piston-powered attack bombers and fighter/bombers. The nature of the Korean terrain rendered some ground targets impervious to high-altitude strategic bombing attacks. In these situations, the propeller-driven Navy planes were called in to destroy the target. Just such a target was the Hwachon Dam.

Earlier attacks by B-29 bombers had failed to knock out this vital Communist supply link. A raid by U.S. Navy Douglas AD Skyraiders on 1 May 1951, however, managed to destroy Hwachon Dam.

Mission Setup.
Select Game Mode.
Press 2.
Choose Skill Level.
Press 0.
Select Aircraft Type.
Press 1.
Select Armament.
Press 3 three times. Total 0.
Press 4 five times. Total 2.
Press 5.

Note: Even though the Hwachon Dam mission was flown by ADs, F9F-2s will be used in this scenario. After all, this is JET.

Your F9F-2 has a top speed of Mach .7 at a maximum altitude of 42,000 feet.

Do not use the Radar System Display, the Weapon Tracking Indicator, or the Attitude Indicator. The afterburner may not be used during this scenario.

Your only armament is four 20mm cannons in your jet's nose and two 500lb bombs.

Mission Objectives. Bomb a surface vessel near Hwachon Dam.

Flying the Mission.
Step 1. Take off from the aircraft carrier.
Step 2. Never exceed an indicated airspeed of Mach .7 or an altitude of 42,000 feet.
Step 3. Activate the M61A1 Weapon System. Fire off 300 rounds of your 500 rounds of ammunition. You now have a total of 200 rounds of machine gun ammunition for combat.
Step 4. Bomb and strafe the surface target until it is destroyed.
Step 5. Return to the aircraft carrier and land.

Mission Debriefing. You will have successfully flown this mission if you:

☐ Stayed within the performance boundaries of the F9F-2.
☐ Sank the target vessel.
☐ Safely completed the mission.

13. CUTTING SUPPLY LINES

Once the Sabre jet began to rule the sky, the now-antiquated F-80C could be used as a strike aircraft. While the Shooting Star had lost its edge in aerial jet combat, it excelled in its new fighter/bomber role. The Communist spring offensive in 1951 demanded constant ground target strikes by the F-80C fighter/bombers. Roads, bridgeheads, fuel depots, and river traffic all fell prey to constant aerial bombardment.

Mission Setup.
Select Game Mode.
Press 2.

Choose Skill Level.

Press 0.

Select Aircraft Type.

Press 2.

Select Armament.

Press 3 three times. Total 0.

Press 4 five times. Total 2.

Press 5.

Your F-80C has a top speed of Mach .7 at a maximum altitude of 42,000 feet.

Do not use the Radar System Display, the Weapon Tracking Indicator, or the Attitude Indicator.

The afterburner may not be used during this scenario.

Your only armament is six .50-caliber M3 machine guns in your jet's nose and two external 500lb bombs.

Mission Objectives. Bomb and strafe the enemy ground target.

Flying the Mission.

Step 1. Take off from runway 22L.

Step 2. Never exceed an indicated airspeed of Mach .7 or an altitude of 42,000 feet.

Step 3. Activate the M61A1 Weapon System. Fire off 300 rounds of your 500 rounds of ammunition. You now have a total of 200 rounds of machine gun ammunition for combat.

Step 4. Locate the ground target (Fig. 6-1).

Step 5. Bomb and strafe the target until it is destroyed.

Step 6. Return to base and land.

Step 7. Taxi into the hangar.

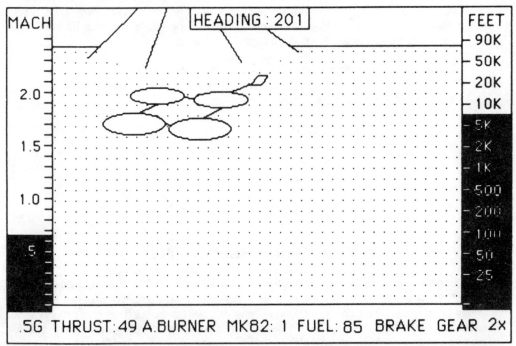

Fig. 6-1. The first pass on this ground target proved unsuccessful. Only one 500lb bomb remains for finishing this mission.

Mission Debriefing. You will have successfully flown this mission if you:

☐ Stayed within the performance boundaries of the F-80C.
☐ Destroyed the enemy ground target.
☐ Safely completed the mission.

14. TROOP MOVEMENTS

As America's involvement in the Korean War increased, new aircraft were designed to meet more specialized needs. More often than not, these new aircraft failed to arrive as quickly as the situation demanded. This operational lag forced the U.S. Air Force to field-modify the mission of many of its now obsolete jets. One of these reclassified jets was the Republic F-84G Thunderjet. The F-84G began the war much like the Shooting Star—an air superiority jet fighter. After the appearance of the MiG-15, however, both the Shooting Star and the Thunderjet were restricted to ground strike missions.

Mission Setup.
Select Game Mode.
Press 2.
Choose Skill Level.
Press 0.
Select Aircraft Type.
Press 2.
Select Armament.
Press 3 three times. Total 0.
Press 4 five times. Total 2.
Press 5.
Your F-84G has a top speed of Mach .8 at a maximum altitude of 40,000 feet.
Do not use the Radar System Display, the Weapon Tracking Indicator, or the Attitude Indicator. The afterburner may not be used during this scenario.
Your only armament is six .50-caliber M3 machine guns (four in the jet's nose and two in the wing roots) and two external 500lb bombs.
Mission Objectives. Bomb and strafe the enemy ground target.
Flying the Mission.
Step 1. Take off from runway 22L.
Step 2. Never exceed an indicated airspeed of Mach .8 or an altitude of 40,000 feet.
Step 3. Activate the M61A1 Weapon System. Fire off 300 rounds of your 500 rounds of ammunition. You now have a total of 200 rounds of machine gun ammunition for combat.
Step 4. Locate the ground target from an altitude of 15,000 feet.
Step 5. Dive on the target. Bomb and strafe it until it is destroyed.
Step 6. Return to base and land.
Step 7. Taxi into the hangar.
Mission Debriefing. You will have successfully flown this mission if you:

☐ Stayed within the performance boundaries of the F-84G.

☐ Destroyed the enemy ground target.
☐ Safely completed the mission.

15. WOLMI DO

During the early days of the Korean war, naval aircraft were called on to support Allied beach assaults. These ground strike missions were similar to those flown five years earlier by U.S. Navy carrier planes in support of World War II Allied island invasions. The amphibious landing at Inchon on 15 September 1950 demonstrated the vital need for strong air support during beach assaults. U.S. Navy F9F-2s flew continuous sorties against Communist positions as U.S. Marines stormed ashore at Wolmi Do. Within several days key positions in South Korea had been reclaimed.

Mission Setup.
Select Game Mode.
Press 2.
Choose Skill Level.
Press 0.
Select Aircraft Type.
Press 1.
Select Armament.
Press 3 three times. Total 0.
Press 4 two times. Total 6.
Press 5.
Your F9F-2 has a top speed of Mach .7 at a maximum altitude of 42,000 feet.
Do not use the Radar System Display, the Weapon Tracking Indicator, or the Attitude Indicator. The afterburner may not be used during this scenario.
Your only armament is four 20mm cannons in your jet's nose and six 500lb bombs.
Mission Objectives. Fly four sorties against Communist vessels near Wolmi Do.
Flying the Mission.
Step 1. Take off from the aircraft carrier.
Step 2. Never exceed an indicated airspeed of Mach .7 or an altitude of 42,000 feet.
Step 3. Activate the M61A1 Weapon System. Fire off 300 rounds of your 500 rounds of ammunition. You now have a total of 200 rounds of machine gun ammunition for combat.
Step 4. Bomb and strafe all vessels of opportunity.
Step 5. Return to the aircraft carrier and land.
Step 6. Repeat this pattern for a total of four sorties.
Mission Debriefing. You will have successfully flown this mission if you:

☐ Stayed within the performance boundaries of the F9F-2.
☐ Flew four sorties.
☐ Sank numerous target vessels.
☐ Safely completed the mission.

16. KIMPO AIRFIELD

The most vital goal during the Inchon invasion was to secure the Kimpo airfield near Seoul. If the Allied forces were able to capture this base, then they would have a secure land airbase for supporting further advances against the retreating Communist forces. Flying F9F-2s, naval pilots were able to provide a constant aerial umbrella for the invading U.S. Marines. Kimpo airfield was occupied by U.S. Marines only eleven days after their landing at Wolmi Do. Soon land-based Marine aircraft were launching from Kimpo to continue the fight to the 38th Parallel.

Mission Setup.

Select Game Mode.
Press 2.

Choose Skill Level.
Press 0.

Select Aircraft Type.
Press 2.

Select Armament.
Press 3 three times. Total 0.
Press 4 two times. Total 6.
Press 5.

Note: Even though you will be flying a Navy jet, you will be taking off from a land base. This will provide greater accuracy in duplicating the F9F-2's ground support role around Kimpo.

Your F9F-2 has a top speed of Mach .7 at a maximum altitude of 42,000 feet.

Do not use the Radar System Display, the Weapon Tracking Indicator, or the Attitude Indicator. The afterburner may not be used during this scenario.

Your only armament is four 20mm cannons in your jet's nose and six 500lb bombs.

Mission Objectives. Fly three sorties against Communist ground targets around Kimpo.

Flying the Mission.

Step 1. Take off from runway 22L.

Step 2. Never exceed an indicated airspeed of Mach .7 or an altitude of 42,000 feet.

Step 3. Activate the M61A1 Weapon System. Fire off 300 rounds of your 500 rounds of ammunition. You now have a total of 200 rounds of machine gun ammunition for combat.

Step 4. Bomb and strafe all ground targets.

Step 5. Return to the airbase, land, and taxi into the hangar.

Step 6. Repeat this pattern for a total of three sorties.

Mission Debriefing. You will have successfully flown this mission if you:

☐ Stayed within the performance boundaries of the F9F-2.
☐ Flew three sorties.
☐ Destroyed numerous ground targets.
☐ Safely completed the mission.

17. THE PUSAN PERIMETER

Simultaneously with the landing at Inchon, Allied troops in the Pusan Perimeter began an attack on the North Korean Army. Slowly two large pincers of advancing troops began to push the Communist forces out of South Korea. This Pusan Perimeter "breakout" was supported by large flights of U.S. naval aircraft. Notably, several waves of F9F-2s provided numerous ground support strikes against the retreating North Korean Army. By 8 October 1950, the U.S. Army was flooding across the 38th Parallel.

Mission Setup.
Select Game Mode.
Press 2.
Choose Skill Level.
Press 0.
Select Aircraft Type.
Press 2.
Select Armament.
Press 3 three times. Total 0.
Press 4 two times. Total 6.
Press 5.

Note: Even though you will be flying a Navy jet, you will be taking off from a land base. This will provide greater accuracy in duplicating the F9F-2s ground support during the Pusan Perimeter breakout.

Your F9F-2 has a top speed of Mach .7 at a maximum altitude of 42,000 feet.

Do not use the Radar System Display, the Weapon Tracking Indicator, or the Attitude Indicator. The afterburner may not be used during this scenario.

Your only armament is four 20mm cannons in your jet's nose and six 500lb bombs.

Mission Objectives. Fly six sorties against Communist ground targets around Kimpo.

Flying the Mission.
Step 1. Take off from runway 22L.
Step 2. Never exceed an indicated airspeed of Mach .7 or an altitude of 42,000 feet.
Step 3. Activate the M61A1 Weapon System. Fire off 300 rounds of your 500 rounds of ammunition. You now have a total of 200 rounds of machine gun ammunition for combat.
Step 4. Bomb and strafe all ground targets.
Step 5. Return to the airbase, land, and taxi into the hangar.
Step 6. Repeat this pattern for a total of six sorties.

Mission Debriefing. You will have successfully flown this mission if you:

☐ Stayed within the performance boundaries of the F9F-2.
☐ Flew six sorties.
☐ Destroyed numerous ground targets.
☐ Flew over the 38th Parallel.
☐ Safely completed the mission.

18. SPRING OFFENSIVE

When the Chinese launched their massive counterinvasion on 26 November 1950, which comprised four massive armies, they wanted to overrun all of Korea. This total occupation would place all of Korea under Communist control. Immediately, under the weight of such an oppressive assault, the greatly outnumbered Allied forces withdrew from North Korea. They established battle lines 25 miles south of Seoul. From airbases deep in South Korea, F-84Gs battled the superior MiG-15s. Luckily for the Communist pilots, the 4th Fighter/Interceptor Wing with their Sabre jets had been withdrawn to Japan. This left only a modest force of Thunderjets for keeping the peace.

Mission Setup.

Select Game Mode.

Press 1.

Choose Skill Level.

Press 1.

Select Aircraft Type.

Press 2.

Select Armament.

Press 1 three times. Total 0.

Press 2 three times. Total 0.

Press 5.

Your F-84G has a top speed of Mach .8 at a maximum altitude of 40,000 feet.

Do not use the Radar System Display, the Weapon Tracking Indicator, or the Attitude Indicator. The afterburner may not be used during this scenario.

Your only armament is six .50-caliber M3 machine guns (four in the jet's nose and two in the wing roots).

Mission Objectives. Shoot down one enemy jet.

Flying the Mission.

Step 1. Take off from runway 22L.

Step 2. Never exceed an indicated airspeed of Mach .8 or an altitude of 40,000 feet.

Step 3. Activate the M61A1 Weapon System. Fire off 300 rounds of your 500 rounds of ammunition. You now have a total of 200 rounds of machine gun ammunition for combat.

Step 4. Climb to 20,000 feet.

Step 5. Attack an enemy jet. The MiG-15 in this scenario has superior performance over your Thunderjet. Therefore, you are extremely susceptible to being shot down. Exercise great caution.

Step 6. Return to base and land.

Step 7. Taxi into the hangar.

Mission Debriefing. You will have successfully flown this mission if you:

☐ Stayed within the performance boundaries of the F-84G.
☐ Destroyed the enemy jet aircraft.
☐ Safely completed the mission.

19. SUWON

Along with the halting of the Communist advance in the spring of 1951, the severe winter weather also left South Korea and the 4th Fighter/Interceptor Wing was able to return from its brief stay in Japan. Upon their return, the Sabre jets again took command of the skies over Korea. Based 40 miles south of Seoul at Suwon, the F-86Es engaged MiG-15s from the 38th Parallel north to the Yalu river. Many of these combats involved large numbers of jets. In each dogfight, however, the Sabre continued to show its excellence.

Mission Setup.

Select Game Mode.

Press 1.

Choose Skill Level.
Press 0.
Select Aircraft Type.
Press 2.
Select Armament.
Press 1 three times. Total 0.
Press 2 three times. Total 0.
Press 5.
Your F-86E has a top speed of Mach .9 at a maximum altitude of 50,000 feet.
Do not use the Radar System Display, the Weapon Tracking Indicator, or the Attitude Indicator.
The afterburner may not be used during this scenario.
Your only armament is six .50-caliber M3 machine guns in your jet's nose.
Mission Objectives. Score ten MiG-15 kills.
Flying the Mission.
Step 1. Take off from runway 22L.
Step 2. Never exceed an indicated airspeed of Mach .9 or an altitude of 50,000 feet.
Step 3. Activate the M61A1 Weapon System. Fire off 300 rounds of your 500 rounds of ammunition. You now have a total of 200 rounds of machine gun ammunition for combat.
Step 4. Intercept and shoot down ten enemy aircraft. In order to bag your MiG limit, you may need to remain on patrol for an extended period of time. Judicious use of the throttle will help to conserve fuel during this mission.
Step 5. Return to base and land.
Step 6. Taxi into the hangar.
Mission Debriefing. You will have successfully flown this mission if you:

☐ Stayed within the performance boundaries of the F-86E.
☐ Shot down all ten of the enemy aircraft with a maximum of 200 rounds of ammunition.
☐ Safely completed the mission.

20. HIGH-ALTITUDE COMBAT

When the Allied army established its final combat lines north of the 38th Parallel, the 4th Fighter/Interceptor Wing was able to move back into Kimpo airfield. From this advanced location, the F-86Es were able to engage and dogfight the MiG-15s for long periods of time. Many times these dogfights raged at extremely high altitudes. This new tactic was brought on by the MiG pilots who were learning the basics of jet fighter combat. Even with these new found dog-fighting skills, the MiG-15s still suffered large losses.
Mission Setup.
Select Game Mode.
Press 1.
Choose Skill Level.
Press 0.
Select Aircraft Type.
Press 2.
Select Armament.
Press 1 three times. Total 0.

Press 2 three times. Total 0.

Press 5.

Your F-86E has a top speed of Mach .9 at a maximum altitude of 50,000 feet.

Do not use the Radar System Display, the Weapon Tracking Indicator, or the Attitude Indicator. The afterburner may not be used during this scenario.

Your only armament is six .50-caliber M3 machine guns in your jet's nose.

Mission Objectives. Score two MiG-15 kills.

Flying the Mission.

Step 1. Take off from runway 22L.

Step 2. Never exceed an indicated airspeed of Mach .9 or an altitude of 50,000 feet.

Step 3. Activate the M61A1 Weapon System. Fire off 300 rounds of your 500 rounds of ammunition. You now have a total of 200 rounds of machine gun ammunition for combat.

Step 4. Climb to an altitude of 40,000 feet.

Step 5. Engage the enemy jets at this altitude.

Step 6. Shoot down two of the jets.

Step 7. Return to base and land.

Step 8. Taxi into the hangar.

Mission Debriefing. You will have successfully flown this mission if you:

☐ Stayed within the performance boundaries of the F-86E.

☐ Intercepted the enemy jets at an altitude of 40,000 feet.

☐ Shot down two of the enemy aircraft with a maximum of 200 rounds of ammunition.

☐ Safely completed the mission.

21. BRIDGE STRIKE

United Nations aircraft carriers played an important role in supporting constant air strikes against the Communist forces north of the 38th Parallel. The Royal Navy carriers *HMS Theseus, HMS Glory,* and *HMS Triumph* launched fighter/bombers such as the Fairey Firefly and Hawker Sea Fury loaded with air-to-ground rockets and bombs for destroying selected ground targets. The American carriers *USS Philippine Sea* and *USS Valley Forge* catapulted F9F-2s intent on severing major supply lines. Many of these Panthers' targets included bridges and their associated river traffic.

Mission Setup.

Select Game Mode.

Press 2.

Choose Skill Level.

Press 0.

Select Aircraft Type.

Press 1.

Select Armament.

Press 3 three times. Total 0.

Press 4 five times. Total 2.

Press 5.

Your F9F-2 has a top speed of Mach .7 at a maximum altitude of 42,000 feet.

Do not use the Radar System Display, the Weapon Tracking Indicator, or the Attitude Indicator.

The afterburner may not be used during this scenario.

Your only armament is four 20mm cannons in your jet's nose and two 500lb bombs.

Mission Objectives. Attack all river traffic.

Flying the Mission.

Step 1. Take off from the aircraft carrier.

Step 2. Never exceed an indicated airspeed of Mach .7 or an altitude of 42,000 feet.

Step 3. Activate the M61A1 Weapon System. Fire off 300 rounds of your 500 rounds of ammunition. You now have a total of 200 rounds of machine gun ammunition for combat.

Step 4. Bomb and strafe all the surface targets that are encountered during patrol.

Step 5. Return to the aircraft carrier and land.

Mission Debriefing. You will have successfully flown this mission if you:

☐ Stayed within the performance boundaries of the F9F-2.

☐ Sank any enemy surface vessels.

☐ Safely completed the mission.

22. ALL-WEATHER COMBAT

The tempermental weather over Korea did more to ground the Allied air forces than all of the aerial escapades of every MiG, Yakovlev, and Ilyushin aircraft combined. What was needed was an all-weather fighter that could operate in virtually any climatic condition. Lockheed was the first aircraft manufacturer to arrive at a solution to this problem. By modifying the structure of the Shooting Star, two new aircraft features could be added to the designated F-94B Starfire. The F-94B's nose-mounted radar system and thrust-increasing afterburner marked the beginning of a new age in jet fighter design.

Mission Setup.

Select Game Mode.

Press 1.

Choose Skill Level.

Press 0.

Select Aircraft Type.

Press 2.

Select Armament.

Press 1 three times. Total 0.

Press 2 three times. Total 0.

Press 5.

Your F-94B has a top speed of Mach .8 at a maximum altitude of 55,000 feet.

Do not use the Weapon Tracking Indicator or the Attitude Indicator.

The afterburner and the Radar System Display may be used during this scenario.

Your only armament is four .50-caliber M3 machine guns in your jet's nose.

Mission Objectives. Score one MiG-15 kill.

Flying the Mission.

Step 1. Take off from runway 22L.

Step 2. Never exceed an indicated airspeed of Mach .8 or an altitude of 55,000 feet.

Step 3. Activate the M61A1 Weapon System. Fire off 300 rounds of your 500 rounds of ammunition. You now have a total of 200 rounds of machine gun ammunition for combat.

Step 4. Climb to an altitude of 20,000 feet.
Step 5. Use your Radar System Display to engage the enemy jet at this altitude.
Step 6. Shoot down the jet.
Step 7. Return to base and land.
Step 8. Taxi into the hangar.
Mission Debriefing. You will have successfully flown this mission if you:

☐ Stayed within the performance boundaries of the F-94B.
☐ Intercepted the enemy jet at an altitude of 20,000 feet.
☐ Shot down one enemy aircraft with a maximum of 200 rounds of ammunition.
☐ Safely completed the mission.

23. YALU RIVER

Throughout the Korean War, one region of aerial battle became the focal point of Allied air superiority. South of the Yalu river and north of Pyongyang, an area frequented by MiG-15 pilots, earned the nickname "MiG Alley." Every major jet dogfight following the stalemate along the 38th Parallel occurred in MiG Alley. The older F-86Es were still able to handle the newer MiG-15s that were beginning to appear. These new MiG-15s, however, possessed several superior flight characteristics that their pilots quickly learned to exploit.
Mission Setup.
Select Game Mode.
Press 1.
Choose Skill Level.
Press 0.
Select Aircraft Type.
Press 2.
Select Armament.
Press 1 three times. Total 0.
Press 2 three times. Total 0.
Press 5.
Your F-86E has a top speed of Mach .9 at a maximum altitude of 50,000 feet.
Do not use the Radar System Display, the Weapon Tracking Indicator, or the Attitude Indicator. The afterburner may not be used during this scenario.
Your only armament is six .50-caliber M3 machine guns in your jet's nose.
Mission Objectives. Fly two sorties and kill 12 MiG-15's.
Flying the Mission.
Step 1. Take off from runway 22L.
Step 2. Never exceed an indicated airspeed of Mach .9 or an altitude of 50,000 feet.
Step 3. Activate the M61A1 Weapon System. Fire off 300 rounds of your 500 rounds of ammunition. You now have a total of 200 rounds of machine gun ammunition for combat.
Step 4. Climb to an altitude of 35,000 feet.
Step 5. Engage the enemy jets at this altitude.
Step 6. Shoot down six MiGs.
Step 7. Return to base and land.
Step 8. Taxi into the hangar.

Step 9. Repeat the above steps for one more sortie.
Mission Debriefing. You will have successfully flown this mission if you:

☐ Stayed within the performance boundaries of the F-86E.
☐ Intercepted the enemy jets at an altitude of 35,000 feet.
☐ Shot down 12 of the enemy aircraft with two sorties.
☐ Safely completed the mission.

24. EASY KILLS

As the Communist pilots learned to exploit the advantages that their new MiG-15bis showed over the aging F-86E, Sabre jet losses began to climb. This superiority was short-lived, however. In the summer of 1952, the 51st Fighter Wing received a gift from the States—the new F-86F had arrived. A newer wing design gave the F-86F excellent performance and maneuverability at high altitudes. Now the Sabre jet could engage and win any type of MiG-15 combat confrontation.

Mission Setup.
Select Game Mode.
Press 1.
Choose Skill Level.
Press 0.
Select Aircraft Type.
Press 2.
Select Armament.
Press 1 three times. Total 0.
Press 2 three times. Total 0.
Press 5.
Your F-86F has a top speed of Mach .9 at a maximum altitude of 50,000 feet.
Do not use the Radar System Display, the Weapon Tracking Indicator, or the Attitude Indicator.
The afterburner may not be used during this scenario.
Your only armament is six .50-caliber M3 machine guns in your jet's nose.
Mission Objectives. Shoot down 10 jets in one sortie.
Flying the Mission.
Step 1. Take off from runway 22L.
Step 2. Never exceed an indicated airspeed of Mach .9 or an altitude of 50,000 feet.
Step 3. Activate the M61A1 Weapon System. Fire off 200 rounds of your 500 rounds of ammunition. You now have a total of 300 rounds of machine gun ammunition for combat.
Step 4. Climb to an altitude of 45,000 feet.
Step 5. Engage the enemy jets at this altitude.
Step 6. Shoot down 10 MiGs.
Step 7. Return to base and land.
Step 8. Taxi into the hangar.
Mission Debriefing. You will have successfully flown this mission if you:

☐ Stayed within the performance boundaries of the F-86F.
☐ Intercepted the enemy jets at an altitude of 45,000 feet.
☐ Shot down 10 of the enemy aircraft.
☐ Safely completed the mission.

25. THE BEGINNING OF MODERN JET WARFARE

American air power became highly advanced at the end of the Korean War. The addition of radar guidance systems and afterburning jet engines marked the birth of a new era in jet fighter design. Another new feature, placed in special F-86Ds, was air-to-air rockets. These 18 pound projectiles could shoot down an enemy jet with just one hit. One tradeoff with the employment of these rockets was the loss of the machine gun and cannon armament. This weapon exclusion would come back to haunt American pilots during the Vietnam War.

Mission Setup.

Select Game Mode.

Press 1.

Choose Skill Level.

Press 1.

Select Aircraft Type.

Press 2.

Select Armament.

Press 1 two times. Total 6.

Press 2 three times. Total 0.

Press 5.

Your F-86D has a top speed of Mach .9 at a maximum altitude of 55,000 feet.

Do not use the Radar System Display or the Attitude Indicator.

The afterburner and the Weapon Tracking Indicator may be used during this scenario.

Your only armament is six air-to-air rockets carried in a ventral tray.

Mission Objectives. Shoot down one enemy aircraft.

Flying the Mission.

Step 1. Take off from runway 22L.

Step 2. Never exceed an indicated airspeed of Mach .9 or an altitude of 55,000 feet.

Step 3. Activate the M61A1 Weapon System. Fire off all 500 rounds of your ammunition. You now have 0 rounds of machine gun ammunition for combat.

Step 4. Climb to an altitude of 50,000 feet.

Step 5. Engage the enemy jet at this altitude.

Step 6. Shoot down the MiG.

Step 7. Return to base and land.

Step 8. Taxi into the hangar.

Mission Debriefing. You will have successfully flown this mission if you:

☐ Stayed within the performance boundaries of the F-86D.

☐ Intercepted the enemy jet at an altitude of 50,000 feet.

☐ Shot down the enemy aircraft.

☐ Safely completed the mission.

Chapter 7

Vietnam War

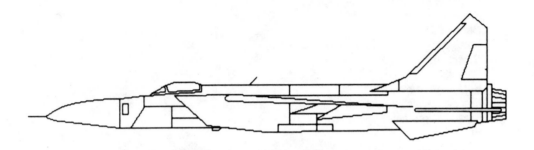

26. FLAMING DART

A Communist infiltration into a democratic state was beginning to stress the United States into its fourth significant war in less than 50 years. South Vietnam had already received several years of limited aid from France. This support ended, however, when the French Army suffered a fatal defeat at Dien Bien Phu in May 1954. Now the United States stepped in to help stem the red tide. Most of the American assistance came from limited air strikes and covert military adviser operations. Four North Vietnamese aggressions finally prodded the U.S. into a larger involvement. Two of these attacks were on U.S. Navy vessels. A naval attack on the *USS Maddox* and the *USS Turner Joy* (coincidentally, Vice Admiral C. Turner Joy led the UN truce talks during the Korean War) resulted in a limited air strike against North Vietnamese targets. A Christmas Eve attack on an American hotel and the bombing of Pleiku airfield initiated a larger air strike. Operation Flaming Dart consisted of several flights of U.S. Navy Douglas A-4E Skyhawk jets bombing Dong Hoi and Vit Thuu. By early March 1965, America was at war again.

    Mission Setup.
    Select Game Mode.
    Press 2.
    Choose Skill Level.
    Press 1.
    Select Aircraft Type.
    Press 1.
    Select Armament.
    Press 3 three times. Total 0.
    Press 4 two times. Total 6.
    Press 5.
    Your A-4E has a top speed of Mach .9 at a maximum altitude of 49,000 feet.

The Radar System Display and Weapon Tracking Indicator may be used during this scenario. The afterburner may not be used.

Your armament is two 20mm cannons mounted in the wing roots and six 500lb bombs carried on external stores.

Mission Objectives. Surprise and destroy a Viet Cong gunboat.

Flying the Mission.

Step 1. Take off from the aircraft carrier.

Step 2. Never exceed an indicated airspeed of Mach .9 or an altitude of 49,000 feet.

Step 3. Climb to an altitude of 30,000 feet.

Step 4. Locate the target on your radar.

Step 5. Bomb and strafe the vessel.

Step 6. Return to the carrier and land.

Mission Debriefing. You will have successfully flown this mission if you:

☐ Stayed within the performance boundaries of the A-4E.
☐ Located and destroyed the VC gunboat from a starting altitude of 30,000 feet.
☐ Safely completed the mission.

27. FLAMING DART II

Operation Flaming Dart did very little to halt the spread of Viet Cong activities and attacks throughout South Vietnam. On 11 February 1965 another air strike was directed at a North Vietnamese target, this time near Chanh Hoa. This operation, known as Flaming Dart II, lacked the credible justification of the original Flaming Dart. In a National Security Action Memorandum, only a vague statement—"continued acts of aggression"—was issued in support of Flaming Dart II. Furthermore, the memo states that " . . . the second Flaming Dart operation . . . set the stage for the continuing bombing program . . . " Unlike Flaming Dart, the second operation used U.S. Air Force as well as Navy aircraft in the attack. North American F-100D Super Sabre jets formed the U.S. Air Force contribution to Flaming Dart II.

Mission Setup.

Select Game Mode.

Press 2.

Choose Skill Level.

Press 1.

Select Aircraft Type.

Press 2.

Select Armament.

Press 3 three times. Total 0.

Press 4 two times. Total 6.

Press 5.

Your F-100D has a top speed of Mach 1.1 at a maximum altitude of 50,000 feet.

The afterburner, Radar System Display, and Weapon Tracking Indicator may be used during this scenario.

Your armament is four 20mm M39E cannons with 200 rounds of ammunition mounted in the jet's nose and six 500lb bombs carried on external stores.

Mission Objectives. Bomb and strafe Chanh Hoa.

Flying the Mission.

Step 1. Take off from runway 0.

Step 2. Never exceed an indicated airspeed of Mach 1.1 or an altitude of 50,000 feet.

Step 3. Climb to an altitude of 25,000 feet.

Step 4. Activate the M61A1 Weapon System. Fire off 300 rounds of your 500 rounds of ammunition. You now have a total of 200 rounds of cannon ammunition for combat.

Step 5. Locate the target on your radar.

Step 6. Bomb and strafe Chanh Hoa.

Step 7. Return to the home base and land.

Step 8. Taxi into the hangar.

Mission Debriefing. You will have successfully flown this mission if you:

☐ Stayed within the performance boundaries of the F-100D.

☐ Located and destroyed Chanh Hoa from a starting altitude of 25,000 feet.

☐ Safely completed the mission.

28. ROLLING THUNDER

In an effort to minimize the number of American ground troops in South Vietnam, President Johnson decided to employ a large-scale bombing operation of North Vietnam. Based chiefly on the candid comments from his strategists (namely Walt Rostow), Johnson notified South Vietnam of the proposed 20 February 1965 start date of Operation Rolling Thunder. A governmental coup attempt, a feared coup attempt, a false alarm, and a monsoon delayed the beginning of Rolling Thunder until 2 March 1965. In the first of many different air strikes, F-100Ds and Republic F-105 Thunderchiefs attacked the ammunition dump at Xombang. Operation Rolling Thunder had finally begun.

Mission Setup.

Select Game Mode.

Press 2.

Choose Skill Level.

Press 1.

Select Aircraft Type.

Press 2.

Select Armament.

Press 3 three times. Total 0.

Press 4 two times. Total 6.

Press 5.

Your F-100D has a top speed of Mach 1.1 at a maximum altitude of 50,000 feet.

The afterburner, Radar System Display, and Weapon Tracking Indicator may be used during this scenario.

Your armament is four 20mm M39E cannons with 200 rounds of ammunition mounted in the jet's nose and six 500lb bombs carried on external stores.

Mission Objectives. Bomb and strafe Xombang.

Flying the Mission.

Step 1. Take off from runway 0.

Step 2. Never exceed an indicated airspeed of Mach 1.1 or an altitude of 50,000 feet.

Step 3. Climb to an altitude of 15,000 feet.

Step 4. Activate the M61A1 Weapon System. Fire off 300 rounds of your 500 rounds of ammunition. You now have a total of 200 rounds of cannon ammunition for combat.

Step 5. Locate the target on your radar.

Step 6. Bomb and strafe the ammunition depot.

Step 7. Return to the home base and land.

Step 8. Taxi into the hangar.

Mission Debriefing. You will have successfully flown this mission if you:

☐ Stayed within the performance boundaries of the F-100D.

☐ Located and destroyed Xombang from a starting altitude of 15,000 feet.

☐ Safely completed the mission.

29. DIXIE STATION

Vietnam's rivers were a useful troop and supply route. Trying to stop the flood of Viet Cong into the South began with the destruction of these vital supply lines. At the heart of these river routes was the Mekong delta. Operating from U.S. Navy aircraft carriers, A-4Es repeatedly hit enemy vessels that were using this important waterway. The staging area for this naval carrier force was code named Dixie Station. Every flight into the loosely defended Mekong delta served as an important combat lesson for the carrier pilots who would soon be flying over North Vietnam.

Mission Setup.

Select Game Mode.

Press 2.

Choose Skill Level.

Press 1.

Select Aircraft Type.

Press 1.

Select Armament.

Press 3 three times. Total 0.

Press 4 two times. Total 6.

Press 5.

Your A-4E has a top speed of Mach .9 at a maximum altitude of 49,000 feet.

The Radar System Display and Weapon Tracking Indicator may be used during this scenario. The afterburner may not be used.

Your only armament is two 20mm cannons mounted in the wing roots and six 500lb bombs carried on external stores.

Mission Objectives. Clean the Mekong delta of VC supply boats.

Flying the Mission.

Step 1. Take off from the aircraft carrier.

Step 2. Never exceed an indicated airspeed of Mach .9 or an altitude of 49,000 feet.

Step 3. Climb to an altitude of 10,000 feet.

Step 4. Locate the target on your radar.

Step 5. Bomb and strafe the vessel.

Step 6. Check your radar for additional targets. Stay on alert in the delta region until all of your offensive weapons have been used.

Step 7. Return to the carrier and land.

Mission Debriefing. You will have successfully flown this mission if you:

☐ Stayed within the performance boundaries of the A-4E.
☐ Located and destroyed all enemy surface traffic on the Mekong delta.
☐ Safely completed the mission.

30. MEKONG DELTA

The U.S. Navy wasn't the only branch of the American air arm to participate in air strikes against river traffic on the Mekong delta. Numerous U.S. Air Force sorties were flown against Viet Cong surface vessels operating along the Mekong's river network. One prominent member within the Air Force's inventory was extremely successful at carrying enough external weapon stores to destroy large numbers of enemy water targets. The Air Force's Republic F-105D Thunderchief became the leading supersonic attack fighter/bomber in the early stages of the Vietnam War. On one mission, an F-105D was capable of lifting more payload than a Boeing B-17G bomber of World War II vintage. Couple this bombing capability with the F-105D's proven MiG-killing talents and here was the king of the Mekong delta.

Mission Setup.
Select Game Mode.
Press 2.
Choose Skill Level.
Press 1.
Select Aircraft Type.
Press 2.
Select Armament.
Press 3 five times. Total 2.
Press 4 two times. Total 6.
Press 5.
Your F-105D has a top speed of Mach 1.8 at a maximum altitude of 50,000 feet.

The afterburner, Radar System Display, and Weapon Tracking Indicator may be used during this scenario.

Your armament is one 20mm M61 cannon with 500 rounds of ammunition mounted in the jet's nose and six 500lb bombs and 2 AGM-12 Bullpup ASMs carried on external stores.

Mission Objectives. Bomb and strafe surface targets near the Mekong delta.
Flying the Mission.
Step 1. Take off from runway 0.
Step 2. Never exceed an indicated airspeed of Mach 1.8 or an altitude of 50,000 feet.
Step 3. Climb to an altitude of 15,000 feet.
Step 4. Locate the target on your radar.
Step 5. Bomb and strafe the target.
Step 6. Return to the home base and land.
Step 7. Taxi into the hangar.

Mission Debriefing. You will have successfully flown this mission if you:

☐ Stayed within the performance boundaries of the F-105D.
☐ Located and destroyed the Mekong delta target from a starting altitude of 15,000 feet.
☐ Safely completed the mission.

31. IRON HAND

When the American air war moved into North Vietnam, the losses of U.S. aircraft increased dramatically. This rise in casualties was not the result of improved Communist fighter activity, rather it was from the accurate nature of the surface-to-air missile (SAM) facilities that blanketed the North. New Soviet SA-2 SAMs ringed each North Vietnamese military target with a curtain of steel. In an effort to crush the SAM threat, special "Wild Weasel" F-105Ds and F-100Ds were developed with an anti-SAM role. Each Thunderchief, for example, carried AGM-45 Shrike ARMs (anti-radiation missiles) which would "home" in on the radar signals used by the SAM site and destroy the ground-based guidance system. These "Wild Weasels" were organized into air units that would fly in at low altitude ahead of the main bombing force. Using the name "Iron Hand," these F-105Ds would attack the SAM sites before they could launch their missiles at the more vulnerable bombers.

Mission Setup.
Select Game Mode.
Press 2.
Choose Skill Level.
Press 5.
Select Aircraft Type.
Press 2.
Select Armament.
Press 3 zero times. Total 4.
Press 4 three times. Total 0.
Press 5.
Your F-105D has a top speed of Mach 1.8 at a maximum altitude of 50,000 feet.
The afterburner, Radar System Display, and Weapon Tracking Indicator may be used during this scenario.
Your armament is one 20mm M61 cannon with 500 rounds of ammunition mounted in the jet's nose and four AGM-45 Shrike ARMs carried on external stores.
Mission Objectives. Knock out the SAM sites prior to the arrival of the main strike force.
Flying the Mission.
Step 1. Take off from runway 0.
Step 2. Never exceed an indicated airspeed of Mach 1.8 or an altitude of 50,000 feet.
Step 3. Climb to an altitude of 15,000 feet.
Step 4. Locate the SAM site or sites on your radar.
Step 5. Fire your Shrikes at the site and destroy it. Evade all enemy SAM fire. Combine your afterburner with high-speed breaking turns to avoid the SAMs. Remember to cut your afterburner as the SAM closes in and then make a sharp high-G turn.
Step 7. Return to the home base and land.
Step 8. Taxi into the hangar.
Mission Debriefing. You will have successfully flown this mission if you:

☐ Stayed within the performance boundaries of the F-105D.
☐ Survived the mission.
☐ Destroyed the SAM site or sites.

32. AIR THUDS

The venerable F-105D wasn't just another powerful bomber in the Air Forces's inventory. By strapping on six AIM-9 Sidewinder AAMs, the F-105D became an air superiority fighter. Nicknamed "Thud," the Thunderchiefs were able to engage and win an aerial duel with a North Vietnamese MiG. Its internal 20mm cannon also came into play during the close combat quarters preferred by the MiG pilots. At least 29 MiG kills were recorded by Thuds over North Vietnam.

Mission Setup.
Select Game Mode.
Press 1.
Choose Skill Level.
Press 2.
Select Aircraft Type.
Press 2.
Select Armament.
Press 1 two times. Total 6.
Press 2 three times. Total 0.
Press 5.
Your F-105D has a top speed of Mach 1.8 at a maximum altitude of 50,000 feet.

The afterburner, Radar System Display, and Weapon Tracking Indicator may be used during this scenario.

Your armament is one 20mm M61 cannon with 500 rounds of ammunition mounted in the jet's nose and six AIM-9 Sidewinder AAMs carried on external stores.

Mission Objectives. Engage and destroy MiGs.
Flying the Mission.
Step 1. Take off from runway 0.
Step 2. Never exceed an indicated airspeed of Mach 1.8 or an altitude of 50,000 feet.
Step 3. Climb to an altitude of 10,000 feet.
Step 4. Locate the MiG or MiGs on your radar.
Step 5. Engage the enemy jets and destroy them with your AIM-9s or cannon fire. Evade all enemy missile fire. High-speed maneuvers are the best method for shaking off a pesky missile. Avoid afterburner use, as this spells almost certain death.
Step 6. Return to the home base and land.
Step 7. Taxi into the hangar.

Mission Debriefing. You will have successfully flown this mission if you:

☐ Stayed within the performance boundaries of the F-105D.
☐ Shot down at least one of the enemy jets.
☐ Safely completed the mission.

33. OPERATION BOLO

A new American jet quickly took over many of the attack and air superiority duties of the A-4Es, F-100Ds, and F-105Ds. The McDonnell F-4 Phantom II found a home with the Air Force, Navy, and Marines. Initially, however, its assigned Air Force ground strike tasks proved more than it was capable of handling. Burdened with enormous 16,000 pound bomb loads, the Phantom

IIs were sitting ducks for SAMs, MiG-17s, MiG-19s, and MiG-21s. Colonel Robin Olds, commander of the 8th Tactical Fighter Wing, also known as the "Wolf Pack," organized a special Phantom II air strike that would reduce the MiG problem. In Operation Bolo on 2 January 1967, flying the same formation and using the same call signs as those normally used by bomb-ladened F-105s, 80 Wolf Pack Phantom IIs surprised a large group of MiGs. Olds and his Sidewinder-armed Wolf Pack destroyed seven of the MiGs.

Mission Setup.
Select Game Mode.
Press 1.
Choose Skill Level.
Press 1.
Select Aircraft Type.
Press 2.
Select Armament.
Press 1 two times. Total 6.
Press 2 three times. Total 0.
Press 5.

Your F-4C has a top speed of Mach 1.9 at a maximum altitude of 71,000 feet.

The afterburner, Radar System Display, and Weapon Tracking Indicator may be used during this scenario.

Your only armament is one 20mm M61 cannon with 500 rounds of ammunition mounted on a centerline pod and six AIM-9 Sidewinder AAMs carried on external stores.

Mission Objectives. Engage and destroy seven MiGs.
Flying the Mission.
Step 1. Take off from runway 0.

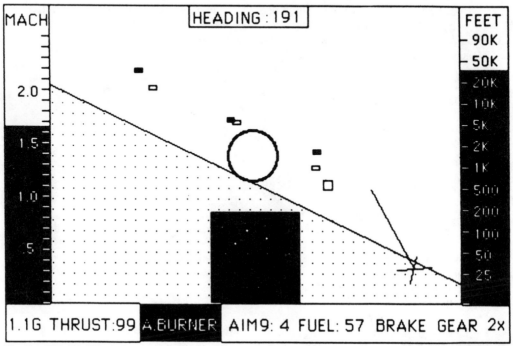

Fig. 7-1. This Wolf Pack F-4 is in trouble. An AIM-9 Sidewinder has just been launched against three firing MiG targets.

Step 2. Never exceed an indicated airspeed of Mach 1.9 or an altitude of 71,000 feet.

Step 3. Climb to an altitude of 20,000 feet.

Step 4. Locate your prey on the radar.

Step 5. Engage the enemy jets and destroy seven of them with your AIM-9s or cannon fire (Fig. 7-1). Evade all enemy missile fire. High-speed maneuvers are the best method for shaking off a pesky missile. Avoid afterburner use, as this spells almost certain death.

Note: For an even more realistic and challenging scenario, try flying the mission without the cannon pod by firing off your 500 rounds of ammunition after Step 2.

Step 6. Return to the home base and land.

Step 7. Taxi into the hangar.

Mission Debriefing. You will have successfully flown this mission if you:

☐ Stayed within the performance boundaries of the F-4C.
☐ Shot down seven of the enemy jets.
☐ Safely completed the mission.

34. MIGCAP

Due to the success of Colonel Olds' Operation Bolo, special interceptor F-4s were used to provide air cover for all bombing missions. These combat air patrol Phantom IIs became MIGCAP fighters. Armed with various combinations of Sidewinder and Sparrow AAMs, the MIGCAP fighters would engage any enemy MiG that ventured near the bombing force. Eventually, the updated F-4E, which carried the M61 cannon internally, appeared. Slowly, the MiG problem began to lessen as the North Vietnamese relied on their SAMs for the defense of their industry.

Mission Setup.

Select Game Mode.

Press 1.

Choose Skill Level.

Press 3.

Select Aircraft Type.

Press 2.

Select Armament.

Press 1 zero times. Total 4.

Press 2 zero times. Total 4.

Press 5.

Your F-4E has a top speed of Mach 1.9 at a maximum altitude of 71,000 feet.

The afterburner, Radar System Display, and Weapon Tracking Indicator may be used during this scenario.

Your armament is one 20mm M61 cannon with 500 rounds of ammunition mounted in the jet's nose and four AIM-9 Sidewinder and four AIM-7D Sparrow III AAMs carried on external stores.

Mission Objectives. Engage and destroy MiGs.

Flying the Mission.

Step 1. Take off from runway 0.

Step 2. Never exceed an indicated airspeed of Mach 1.9 or an altitude of 71,000 feet.

Step 3. Climb to an altitude of 20,000 feet.

Step 4. Locate your prey on the radar.

Step 5. Engage the enemy jets and shoot them down with your AIM-9s, AIM-7Ds, or cannon fire. Evade all enemy missile fire. High-speed maneuvers are the best method for shaking off a pesky missile. Avoid afterburner use, as this spells almost certain death.

Step 6. Return to the home base and land.

Step 7. Taxi into the hangar.

Mission Debriefing. You will have successfully flown this mission if you:

☐ Stayed within the performance boundaries of the F-4E.

☐ Intercepted and shot down any enemy jets.

☐ Safely completed the mission.

35. HO CHI MINH TRAIL

By the mid-1960s, sending Viet Cong supplies through the vast network of Vietnam's waterways had become extremely hazardous. Land-based Air Force and Marine jets continually patrolled these rivers in search of some easy kills. Even Navy aircraft found good hunting around the Mekong delta while at Dixie Station. Faced with a restricted supply line, the Viet Cong placed the Ho Chi Minh Trail into full-scale use. This land artery lacked all of the sophistication that is usually associated with a major western highway; it was just a mass of disjointed dirt roads winding through a dense jungle forest. In spite of its primitive construction, the Ho Chi Minh Trail fed the North's infiltration into the South. In order to stop this arms flow, night mission F-4Es raided the Trail with varying results.

Mission Setup.

Select Game Mode.

Press 2.

Choose Skill Level.

Press 1.

Select Aircraft Type.

Press 2.

Select Armament.

Press 3 zero times. Total 4.

Press 4 zero times. Total 4.

Press 5.

Your F-4E has a top speed of Mach 1.9 at a maximum altitude of 71,000 feet.

The afterburner, Radar System Display, and Weapon Tracking Indicator may be used during this scenario.

Your only armament is one 20mm M61A1 cannon with 500 rounds of ammunition mounted in the jet's nose and four MK-84 500lb bombs and four AGM-12 Bullpup ASMs carried on external stores.

Mission Objectives. Search and destroy all ground targets along the Ho Chi Minh Trail.

Flying the Mission.

Step 1. Take off from runway 0.

Step 2. Never exceed an indicated airspeed of Mach 1.9 or an altitude of 71,000 feet.

Step 3. Climb to an altitude of 20,000 feet.

Step 4. Locate the ground target on your radar.

Step 5. Make your bombing run. Evade all enemy SAM fire. High-speed maneuvers are the best method for shaking off a closing SAM. Avoid afterburner use, as this spells almost certain death.

Step 6. Return to the home base and land.

Step 7. Taxi into the hangar.

Mission Debriefing. You will have successfully flown this mission if you:

☐ Stayed within the performance boundaries of the F-4E.
☐ Located and destroyed the Ho Chi Minh Trail target.
☐ Safely completed the mission.

36. LINEBACKER

In early 1972, many of the American aircrews and their planes had been rotated back to the States. A scheduled pause in the bombing of North Vietnam had necessitated this withdrawal. North Vietnam's massive spring offensive demanded the immediate return of all Navy and Air Force air crews, however. In an effort to halt the delivery of the supplies that supported North Vietnam's General Giap's 14 invading divisions, President Nixon ordered a concentrated bombing of North Vietnamese targets. Operation Linebacker sent a force of 200 B-52Ds and B-52Gs against the North's major industrial centers. "Wild Weasel" and MIGCAP F-4Es flew ahead of the bombers trying to lessen the intensity of the SAM and MiG response.

Mission Setup.

Select Game Mode.

Press 2.

Choose Skill Level.

Press 4.

Select Aircraft Type.

Press 2.

Select Armament.

Press 3 two times. Total 6.

Press 4 zero times. Total 4.

Press 5.

Your F-4E has a top speed of Mach 1.9 at a maximum altitude of 71,000 feet.

The afterburner, Radar System Display, and Weapon Tracking Indicator may be used during this scenario.

Your armament is one 20mm M61A1 cannon with 500 rounds of ammunition mounted in the jet's nose and four MK-84 500lb bombs and four AGM-12 Bullpup ASMs carried on external stores.

Mission Objectives. Destroy all SAM and AAA sites ahead of attacking B-52G's.

Flying the Mission.

Step 1. Take off from runway 0.

Step 2. Never exceed an indicated airspeed of Mach 1.9 or an altitude of 71,000 feet.

Step 3. Climb to an altitude of 20,000 feet.

Step 4. Locate the SAM or AAA site on your radar.

Step 5. Make your bombing run. Evade all enemy SAM fire. High-speed maneuvers are the best method for shaking off a closing SAM. Avoid afterburner use, as this spells almost certain death.

Step 6. Return to the home base and land.

Step 7. Taxi into the hangar.

Mission Debriefing. You will have successfully flown this mission if you:

☐ Stayed within the performance boundaries of the F-4E.
☐ Silenced all SAM and AAA sites.
☐ Safely completed the mission.

37. LINEBACKER II

Operation Linebacker began in June 1972 and ended in October of the same year. The faint belief that the North Vietnamese would concede to a series of peace talks halted Linebacker. Once again, after being deceived by the Communists, Nixon restarted the heavy bombing of North Vietnam. Operation Linebacker II, which started in December 1972, systematically leveled Hanoi and Haiphong. Over 700 B-52G sorties were flown in a short 11-day period following the start of Linebacker II. Unfortunately for the bomber crews, China and Russia had completely resupplied North Vietnam with SAMs and MiG fighters. This time when the "Wild Weasel" and MIGCAP F-4Es made their first pass, the sky lit up with SAMs and MiGs.

Mission Setup.
Select Game Mode.
Press 2.
Choose Skill Level.
Press 6.
Select Aircraft Type.
Press 2.
Select Armament.
Press 3 two times. Total 6.
Press 4 zero times. Total 4.
Press 5.

Your F-4E has a top speed of Mach 1.9 at a maximum altitude of 71,000 feet.

The afterburner, Radar System Display, and Weapon Tracking Indicator may be used during this scenario.

Your only armament is one 20mm M61A1 cannon with 500 rounds of ammunition mounted in the jet's nose and four MK-84 500lb bombs and six AGM-45 Shrike ARMs carried on external stores.

Mission Objectives. Destroy all SAM and AAA sites ahead of attacking B-52G's.

Flying the Mission.

Step 1. Take off from runway 0.

Step 2. Never exceed an indicated airspeed of Mach 1.9 or an altitude of 71,000 feet.

Step 3. Climb to an altitude of 10,000 feet. Combine high speed with a low altitude and try and surprise the enemy (Fig. 7-2).

Step 4. Locate the SAM or AAA site on your radar. Remember these are fresh units. Their equipment is new and their degree of training is high.

Step 5. Make your bombing run. Evade all enemy SAM fire. High-speed maneuvers are the best method for shaking off a closing SAM. Avoid afterburner use, as this spells almost certain death.

Step 6. Return to the home base and land.

Fig. 7-2. "Putting the coal to it," a low-altitude F-4E engaging the afterburners.

Step 7. Taxi into the hangar.

Mission Debriefing. You will have successfully flown this mission if you:

☐ Stayed within the performance boundaries of the F-4E.
☐ Silenced all SAM and AAA sites.
☐ Safely completed the mission. This could be the real test of this scenario. For example, on a single Linebacker II mission, 15 B-52Gs were shot down and another 14 were damaged.

38. PROUD DEEP

While the Linebacker operations had a more strategic scope, a smaller tactical bombing of North Vietnam had already been conducted one year earlier. The results from this operation were less decisive than the 1972 air campaigns, however. This was mainly due to the employment of a ridiculous target restriction plan which isolated both Hanoi and Haiphong from attack. Operation Proud Deep took Air Force and Navy jets against remote supply depots hidden in the country-side. For the most part, the destruction of these targets took a far greater toll on the participating aircraft. The U.S. Navy suffered the greatest, with over 20 aircraft shot down during a five-day period.

    Mission Setup.
    Select Game Mode.
    Press 2.
    Choose Skill Level.
    Press 7.
    Select Aircraft Type.

Press 1.

Select Armament.

Press 3 two times. Total 6.

Press 4 two times. Total 6.

Press 5.

Your F-4J has a top speed of Mach 2 at a maximum altitude of 70,000 feet.

The afterburner, Radar System Display, and Weapon Tracking Indicator may be used during this scenario.

Your armament is six MK-84 500lb bombs and 6 AGM-45 Shrike ARMs carried on external stores.

Mission Objectives. Destroy all SAM sites and supply storage areas.

Flying the Mission.

Step 1. Take off from the aircraft carrier USS Constellation.

Step 2. Never exceed an indicated airspeed of Mach 2 or an altitude of 70,000 feet.

Step 3. Activate the M61A1 Weapon System. Fire off all 500 rounds of your ammunition. You now have 0 rounds of cannon ammunition for combat. The Navy's F-4J was not equipped with an internal cannon.

Step 4. Climb to an altitude of 12,000 feet. All bomb runs will be conducted in level flight from this fixed altitude.

Step 5. After all of the bombs have been dropped, use the AGM-45s in shallow dives on the SAM sites.

Step 6. Evade all enemy SAM fire. High-speed maneuvers are the best method for shaking off a closing SAM. Avoid afterburner use, as this spells almost certain death.

Step 7. Return to the carrier and land.

Mission Debriefing. You will have successfully flown this mission if you:

☐ Stayed within the performance boundaries of the F-4J.

☐ Destroyed all ground targets from an altitude of 12,000 feet. During Proud Deep this altitude was used to avoid heavy overcast that covered the targets. Viet Cong SAM gunners had a "turkey shoot" downing the Navy planes that dropped their bombs from this fixed altitude.

☐ Safely completed the mission. Good luck.

39. VF-90 MIG KILL

An increase in MiG activity in early 1972 forced the U.S. Navy into an offense against this menace. Flying special decoy missions, large flights of naval F-4Js, A-6As, and A-7Es would fly into Laos and turn north into the MiG bases of North Vietnam. Splitting into several attack formations, the Navy fighters would systematically bomb numerous MiG airfields. Naval MIGCAP fighters watched for any scrambled MiGs. Once a MiG became airborne, lengthy dogfights would break out. Near Quan Lang, an attack on a North Vietnamese airbase filled the air with MiG-21s. F-4Js from the *USS Constellation*'s VF-96 engaged the MiGs with Lt. Randy Cunningham downing a MiG-21.

Mission Setup.

Select Game Mode.

Press 1.

Choose Skill Level.
Press 2.
Select Aircraft Type.
Press 1.
Select Armament.
Press 1 zero times. Total 4.
Press 2 three times. Total 0.
Press 5.
Your F-4J has a top speed of Mach 2 at a maximum altitude of 70,000 feet.
The afterburner, Radar System Display, and Weapon Tracking Indicator may be used during this scenario.
Your only armament is four AIM-9D Sidewinder AAMs carried on external stores.
Mission Objectives. Shoot down one MiG-21.
Flying the Mission.
Step 1. Take off from the aircraft carrier *USS Constellation.*
Step 2. Never exceed an indicated airspeed of Mach 2 or an altitude of 70,000 feet.
Step 3. Activate the M61A1 Weapon System. Fire off all 500 rounds of your ammunition. You now have 0 rounds of cannon ammunition for combat. The Navy's F-4J was not equipped with an internal cannon.
Step 4. Climb to an altitude of 15,000 feet.
Step 5. Locate and engage the enemy MiG on your radar.
Step 6. Evade all enemy missile fire. High-speed maneuvers are the best method for shaking off a MiG AAM. Avoid afterburner use, as this spells almost certain death. Shoot down the MiG.
Step 7. Return to the carrier perform one victory roll and land.
Mission Debriefing. You will have successfully flown this mission if you:

☐ Stayed within the performance boundaries of the F-4J.
☐ Shot down one MiG.
☐ Safely completed the mission.

40. COLONEL TOMB

The North Vietnamese MiG drivers weren't without their fair share of American aircraft kills. Several of these Communist pilots became aerial aces in their own right. Two of the better known were Nguyen Van Bay and Colonel Tomb. Van Bay was one of North Vietnam's first aces, with seven American aircraft kills to his credit. Ahead of Van Bay, the leading North Vietnamese ace was Colonel Tomb (this name was an alias used by naval pilots). Tomb had 13 American kills when he met his match on 10 May 1972 at the hands of VF-96 pilot Randy Cunningham. Although the exact fate of Tomb can't be sealed with Cunningham's three MiG kills on May 10th, many believe that "Duke" (Lt. Cunningham's nickname) downed Tomb.
Mission Setup.
Select Game Mode.
Press 1.
Choose Skill Level.
Press 2.
Select Aircraft Type.

Press 1.

Select Armament.

Press 1 zero times. Total 4.

Press 2 five times. Total 2.

Press 5.

Your F-4J has a top speed of Mach 2 at a maximum altitude of 70,000 feet.

The afterburner, Radar System Display, and Weapon Tracking Indicator may be used during this scenario.

Your only armament is four AIM-9D Sidewinder and two AIM-7E Sparrow AAMs carried on external stores.

Mission Objectives. Shoot down three MiGs.

Flying the Mission.

Step 1. Take off from the aircraft carrier *USS Constellation*.

Step 2. Never exceed an indicated airspeed of Mach 2 or an altitude of 70,000 feet.

Step 3. Activate the M61A1 Weapon System. Fire off all 500 rounds of your ammunition. You now have 0 rounds of cannon ammunition for combat. The Navy's F-4J was not equipped with an internal cannon.

Step 4. Climb to an altitude of 10,000 feet.

Step 5. Locate and engage the enemy MiGs on your radar. Be careful with these MiGs, as Colonel Tomb is a skillful pilot.

Step 6. Evade all enemy missile fire. High-speed maneuvers are the best method for shaking off a MiG AAM. Avoid afterburner use, as this spells almost certain death. Shoot down three MiGs.

Step 7. Return to the carrier and land.

Mission Debriefing. You will have successfully flown this mission if you:

☐ Stayed within the performance boundaries of the F-4J.

☐ Shot down three MiGs. Downing these three MiGs made Lt. Cunningham the first American ace during the Vietnam War.

☐ Safely completed the mission. If you achieve this point, then you will have done better than Lt. Cunningham. In his engagement with Colonel Tomb, Cunningham's F-4J was shot down.

41. RED RIVER VALLEY

Some of the most intense aerial encounters between MiGs and Phantom IIs occurred during the flights over Hanoi. The Navy's staging area was often at the mouth of the Red River near Nam Dinh. This whole region was littered with MiG airfields and SAM installations. Flights through the Red River Valley always brought up scores of SAMs, followed by MiG-17 and MiG-19 jet fighters. Many times the bulkier F-4Js had trouble dogfighting the more maneuverable MiG-17s and MiG-19s. This is the time when most Phantom II pilots wished that they had washed out of naval flight school.

Mission Setup.

Select Game Mode.

Press 1.

Choose Skill Level.

Press 4.

Select Aircraft Type.

Press 1.

Select Armament.

Press 1 two times. Total 6.

Press 2 two times. Total 6.

Press 5.

Your F-4J has a top speed of Mach 2 at a maximum altitude of 70,000 feet.

The afterburner, Radar System Display, and Weapon Tracking Indicator may be used during this scenario.

Your armament is six AIM-9D Sidewinder and six AIM-7E Sparrow AAMs carried on external stores.

Mission Objectives. Go MiG hunting.

Flying the Mission.

Step 1. Take off from the aircraft carrier *USS Constellation*.

Step 2. Never exceed an indicated airspeed of Mach 2 or an altitude of 70,000 feet.

Step 3. Activate the M61A1 Weapon System. Fire off all 500 rounds of your ammunition. You now have 0 rounds of cannon ammunition for combat. The Navy's F-4J was not equipped with an internal cannon.

Step 4. Climb to an altitude of 27,000 feet.

Step 5. Locate and engage any enemy MiGs on your radar.

Step 6. Evade all enemy missile fire. High-speed maneuvers are the best method for shaking off a MiG AAM. Avoid afterburner use, as this spells almost certain death. Shoot any MiGs that present themselves.

Step 7. Return to the carrier and land.

Mission Debriefing. You will have successfully flown this mission if you:

☐ Stayed within the performance boundaries of the F-4J.

☐ Shot down any MiGs.

☐ Safely completed the mission.

42. BUF

Of all of the American aircraft to fly over North Vietnam, only the Boeing B-52G Stratofortress placed fear in both the North Vietnamese military and civilian populations. Waves of B-52Gs pounding Hanoi and Haiphong in 1972 eventually contributed to the resumption of peace talks. These enormous flights were not without their share of significant losses, however. During Linebacker II, for example, 15 B-52Gs were shot down over Hanoi. In spite of this high mortality rate, U.S. Air Force aircrews remained loyal to their beloved BUF (an acronym for Big Ugly @*$!).

Mission Setup.

Select Game Mode.

Press 2.

Choose Skill Level.

Press 5.

Select Aircraft Type.

Press 2.

Select Armament.

Press 3 two times. Total 6.

Press 4 two times. Total 6.

Press 5.

Your B-52G has a top speed of Mach .8 at a maximum altitude of 55,000 feet.

The Radar System Display and Weapon Tracking Indicator may be used during this scenario. The afterburner may not be used.

Your only armament is six 1,000lb bombs carried on external stores and six AGM-12 Bullpup ASMs carried in the internal bomb bay.

Mission Objectives. Act like a B-52G and bomb Hanoi.

Flying the Mission.

Step 1. Take off from runway 0.

Step 2. Never exceed an indicated airspeed of Mach .8 or an altitude of 55,000 feet.

Step 3. Climb to an altitude of 40,000 feet.

Step 4. Activate the M61A1 Weapon System. Fire off all 500 rounds of ammunition. You will not be dogfighting with your B-52G.

Step 5. Locate the target on your radar.

Step 6. Remain in level flight at 40,000 feet and release all ordnance.

Step 7. Exit the target area.

Step 8. Land at the home base.

Step 9. Taxi into the hangar.

Mission Debriefing. You will have successfully flown this mission if you:

☐ Stayed within the performance boundaries of the B-52G.

☐ Located and destroyed the target from level flight at 40,000 feet.

☐ Safely completed the mission. This will be extremely difficult considering the density of SAMs located around the target. You will wish you had a squadron of ''Wild Weasel'' fighters flying ahead of you by the time you reach the drop zone.

43. CORSAIR COVER

While the A-4E had started the war as the Navy's leading attack aircraft, MiG and SAM intensity was forcing the small Skyhawks into a more restrained role. Picking up the slack was a new aircraft from LTV Aerospace (Vought). The A-7E Corsair II not only handled attack missions, but it was also capable at being a MIGCAP fighter. A-7Es were also used for Iron Hand duties around targets with large concentrations of SAM installations. This mission diversity made the A-7E useful in being applied to two different tasks on the same sortie. Therefore, after delivering its payload, Corsair IIs were then able to join F-4Js in hunting MiGs.

Mission Setup.

Select Game Mode.

Press 2.

Choose Skill Level.

Press 3.

Select Aircraft Type.

Press 1.

Select Armament.

Press 3 two times. Total 6.

Press 4 two times. Total 6.

Press 5.

Your A-7E has a top speed of Mach .9 at a maximum altitude of 50,000 feet.

The Radar System Display and Weapon Tracking Indicator may be used during this scenario.

The afterburner may not be used with the A-7E.

Your armament is one 20mm M61A1 cannon with 500 rounds of ammunition mounted in the jet's nose and six 500lb MK-82 bombs and six AGM-45 Shrike ARMs carried on external stores.

Mission Objectives. Attack shipping in Haiphong harbor.

Flying the Mission.

Step 1. Take off from the aircraft carrier *USS Kitty Hawk*.

Step 2. Never exceed an indicated airspeed of Mach .9 or an altitude of 50,000 feet.

Step 3. Climb to an altitude of 20,000 feet.

Step 4. Locate the vessels on your radar.

Step 5. Drop your payload on the ships. Attack any other ship that fires on you. Evade all enemy SAM fire.

Step 6. Return to *USS Kitty Hawk* and land.

Mission Debriefing. You will have successfully flown this mission if you:

☐ Stayed within the performance boundaries of the A-7E.

☐ Attacked and sank any enemy ships in the harbor.

☐ Safely completed the mission.

44. INTRUDERS

Along with the Corsair II, the Navy also received the Grumman A-6A Intruder as a substitute for the Skyhawk. While the A-7E was flexible in its assigned mission, the Intruder was a dedicated attack aircraft (there were tanker, reconnaissance, and electronic warfare Intruder versions). Basically, the ability to deliver 15,000 pounds of ordnance at a speed of over 600 mph made the A-6A a potent ground strike weapon. The first use of Intruders was with the VF-75 on *USS Independence*. Used primarily in low-altitude, high-speed bombing runs, the A-6A received the nickname ''Baby B-52'' due to its incredible bomb load delivery ability.

Mission Setup.

Select Game Mode.

Press 2.

Choose Skill Level.

Press 2.

Select Aircraft Type.

Press 1.

Select Armament.

Press 3 three times. Total 0.

Press 4 two times. Total 6.

Press 5.

Your A-6A has a top speed of Mach .9 at a maximum altitude of 47,000 feet.

The Radar System Display and Weapon Tracking Indicator may be used during this scenario.

The afterburner may not be used with the A-6A.

Your only armament is six 1,000lb MK-84 bombs carried on external stores.

Mission Objectives. Search and destroy Viet Cong shipping.

Flying the Mission.

Step 1. Take off from the aircraft carrier *USS Independence.*

Step 2. Never exceed an indicated airspeed of Mach .9 or an altitude of 47,000 feet.

Step 3. Climb to an altitude of 5,000 feet.

Step 4. Locate the vessels on your radar.

Step 5. Dive for a low-altitude, high-speed bombing run. Drop your payload on the ships.

Step 6. Return to *USS Independence* and land.

Mission Debriefing. You will have successfully flown this mission if you:

☐ Stayed within the performance boundaries of the A-6A.

☐ Attacked and sank any enemy ships with a low-altitude, high-speed bombing run.

☐ Safely completed the mission.

45. YANKEE STATION

At the conclusion of the Vietnam War, the U.S. Navy had the bulk of its aircraft carriers committed to positions in the Gulf of Tonkin. From this location, code named Yankee Station, naval aircraft could strike targets throughout North Vietnam. Sitting several miles off the coast of North Vietnam, intense air strikes were mounted around the clock in 1973. Combining the Air Force's Linebacker II B-52G strikes with the Navy's Linebacker II contributions quickly brought the Vietnam War to an end.

A sad footnote to the success of the Yankee Station sorties was the two final naval operations that originated from this former happy hunting ground. First, U.S. Navy helicopters were ordered to clear Haiphong harbor of all American mines. Later, in 1975, aircraft carriers were used to receive South Vietnamese who attempted to flee the bloody North Vietnamese takeover of Saigon.

Mission Setup.

Select Game Mode.

Press 1.

Choose Skill Level.

Press 3.

Select Aircraft Type.

Press 1.

Select Armament.

Press 1 two times. Total 6.

Press 2 five times. Total 2.

Press 5.

Your F-8E has a top speed of Mach 1.4 at a maximum altitude of 58,000 feet.

The afterburner, Radar System Display, and Weapon Tracking Indicator may be used during this scenario.

Your armament is four 20mm Colt MK12 cannons with 500 rounds of ammunition mounted in the jet's nose and six AIM-9 Sidewinder and two AIM-7E Sparrow AAMs carried on external stores.

Mission Objectives. Provide air defense cover for the Saigon evacuation.

‹

Flying the Mission.

Step 1. Take off from the aircraft carrier *USS Coral Sea.*

Step 2. Never exceed an indicated airspeed of Mach 1.4 or an altitude of 58,000 feet.

Step 3. Climb to an altitude of 20,000 feet.

Step 4. Monitor air traffic in the region on your radar.

Step 5. Attack any aircraft that fires on you. Evade all enemy missile fire.

Step 6. Return to *USS Coral Sea* and land.

Mission Debriefing. You will have successfully flown this mission if you:

☐ Stayed within the performance boundaries of the F-8E.

☐ Attacked and shot down any aircraft that attacked you.

☐ Safely completed the mission.

Chapter 8

Current Crises

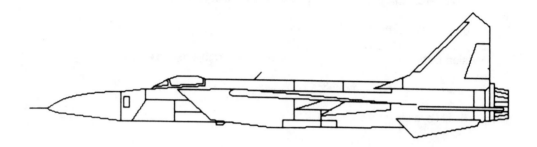

46. THE SIX-DAY WAR

Tensions between Israel and Egypt escalated when the Gulf of Aqaba was closed to Israeli shipping. In response, on 5 June 1967, Israeli aircraft destroyed over 300 Egyptian aircraft in a coordinated series of precision air strikes. Flying Dassault-Breguet Mirage IIICJ jets, Israel commanded the skies over the battle zone. Marching into the Golan Heights, the Israeli army was continually supported by strike aircraft under the cover of air superiority fighters. Whenever Egypt did mount a few MiG-21s for aerial combat, the superior Mirage numbers swamped the MiGs and shot them down. Even though the Arab forces had halted their combat activities on 8 June 1967, the Israelis continued their aggression until all territory objectives had been occupied.

 Mission Setup.
 Select Game Mode.
 Press 2.
 Choose Skill Level.
 Press 1.
 Select Aircraft Type.
 Press 2.
 Select Armament.
 Press 3 two times. Total 6.
 Press 4 two times. Total 6.
 Press 5.
 Your Mirage IIICJ has a top speed of Mach 1.8 at a maximum altitude of 59,000 feet.
 The afterburner, Radar System Display, and Weapon Tracking Indicator may be used during this scenario.
 Your armament is two 30mm DEFA 552 cannons with 200 rounds of ammunition mounted in the jet's nose and six 882lb bombs and six AS.37 Martel ARMs carried on external stores.

Mission Objectives. Destroy all Egyptian targets.

Flying the Mission.

Step 1. Take off from runway 22L.

Step 2. Never exceed an indicated airspeed of Mach 1.8 or an altitude of 59,000 feet.

Step 3. Climb to an altitude of 15,000 feet.

Step 4. Activate the M61A1 Weapon System. Fire off 300 rounds of your ammunition. You now have 200 rounds of cannon ammunition for combat.

Step 5. Locate the target on your radar.

Step 6. Make your bombing run. Evade all enemy SAM fire. High-speed maneuvers are the best method for shaking off a closing SAM. Avoid afterburner use, as this spells almost certain death.

Step 7. Return to the home base and land.

Step 8. Taxi into the hangar.

Mission Debriefing. You will have successfully flown this mission if you:

☐ Stayed within the performance boundaries of the Mirage IIICJ.

☐ Destroyed all ground targets.

☐ Safely completed the mission.

47. YOM KIPPUR WAR

The Israeli occupation of the Sinai had stressed Egypt to a stated war of liberation on 6 October 1973. This outright invasion by Egypt was preceded by large armor buildups and huge artillery barrages. Israel had been caught unprepared by this aggressive move, and quick retaliation was planned on both the ground and in the air. Israeli A-4Es provided ground strikes against the advancing Egyptian 3rd Army, while F-4E Phantom IIs engaged the Egyptian MiGs. MiG-17s, MiG-21PFs, and Su-7BMs were used constantly against the A-4Es and the F-4Es. A turning point in war for Egypt was losing the 14 October tank battle in the Sinai. This loss drained all of Egypt's frontline units, necessitating the second Egyptian surrender in six years on 24 October.

Mission Setup.

Select Game Mode.

Press 1.

Choose Skill Level.

Press 1.

Select Aircraft Type.

Press 2.

Select Armament.

Press 1 two times. Total 6.

Press 2 two times. Total 6.

Press 5.

Your F-4E has a top speed of Mach 1.9 at a maximum altitude of 71,000 feet.

The afterburner, Radar System Display, and Weapon Tracking Indicator may be used during this scenario.

Your armament is one 20mm M61 cannon with 500 rounds of ammunition mounted in the jet's nose and six AIM-9 Sidewinder and six AIM-7D Sparrow III AAMs carried on external stores.

Mission Objectives. Engage and destroy Egyptian MiGs.

Flying the Mission.

Step 1. Take off from runway 22L.

Step 2. Never exceed an indicated airspeed of Mach 1.9 or an altitude of 71,000 feet.

Step 3. Climb to an altitude of 40,000 feet.

Step 4. Locate your victims on the radar.

Step 5. Engage the enemy jets and shoot them down with your AIM-9s, AIM-7Ds, or cannon fire. Evade all enemy missile fire. High-speed maneuvers are the best method for shaking off a pesky missile. Avoid afterburner use, as this spells almost certain death.

Step 7. Return to the home base, execute a victory roll for each downed MiG and land.

Step 8. Taxi into the hangar.

Mission Debriefing. You will have successfully flown this mission if you:

☐ Stayed within the performance boundaries of the F-4E.

☐ Intercepted and shot down any enemy jets.

☐ Safely completed the mission.

48. LEBANON AIR STRIKE

Facing a rise in PLO (Palestine Liberation Organization) terrorist activities, the Israeli government launched a series of air strikes against suspected PLO guerrilla strongholds in Beirut. Using seven waves of General Dynamics F-16A Fighting Falcons, Israel bombed the PLO Beirut headquarters on 2 June 1982. Following this attack, the PLO mounted an artillery barrage against Israeli targets. One thing lead to another and Israel invaded Lebanon on 6 June 1982. Syria immediately lent its support to the PLO cause and provided military hardware in the hope of preventing a complete Israeli takeover. Flying F-16As and McDonnell Douglas F-15A Eagles, the Israelis were able to defeat the Syrian MiG-21s and MiG-23s with regularity. Finally, after a two-year occupation of Lebanon, Israel withdrew its forces with very little real victory.

Mission Setup.

Select Game Mode.

Press 2.

Choose Skill Level.

Press 1.

Select Aircraft Type.

Press 2.

Select Armament.

Press 3 two times. Total 6.

Press 4 two times. Total 6.

Press 5.

Your F-16A has a top speed of Mach 2 at a maximum altitude of 60,000 feet.

The afterburner, Radar System Display, and Weapon Tracking Indicator may be used during this scenario.

Your armament is one 20mm M61A1 cannon with 500 rounds of ammunition mounted in the jet's nose and six MK-82 500lb bombs and six AGM-65E Maverick ASMs carried on external stores.

Mission Objectives. Locate and destroy the PLO HQ.

Flying the Mission.

Step 1. Take off from runway 18.

Step 2. Never exceed an indicated airspeed of Mach 2 or an altitude of 60,000 feet.

Step 3. Climb to an altitude of 20,000 feet.

Step 4. Locate the PLO HQ on your radar.

Step 5. Make your bombing run. Evade all enemy SAM fire.

Step 6. Return to the home base and land.

Step 7. Taxi into the hangar.

Mission Debriefing. You will have successfully flown this mission if you:

☐ Stayed within the performance boundaries of the F-16A.

☐ Located and destroyed the PLO HQ.

☐ Safely completed the mission.

49. BOMBING BENGHAZI

Terrorists reared their ugly heads once too often in early 1986. Using sophisticated intelligence gathering techniques, the U.S. determined that Colonel Muammar Qaddafi of Libya had a hand in most of the terrorist funding and training. In an effort to suppress this illicit support, U.S. Navy aircraft carriers launched a surprise air strike against Benina airfield and Al Jumahiriya barracks near Benghazi, Libya, on 15 April 1986. McDonnell Douglas F/A-18A Hornets and A-7Es operated in a SAM supression role, while A-6Es bombed the ground targets. Grumman F-14A Tomcats and F/A-18As were used as MIGCAP fighters. The total success of this naval strike was the first major aerial victory for the U.S. Navy since the completion of the Linebacker II operations in North Vietnam.

Mission Setup.

Select Game Mode.

Press 2.

Choose Skill Level.

Press 1.

Select Aircraft Type.

Press 1.

Select Armament.

Press 3 two times. Total 6.

Press 4 three times. Total 0.

Press 5.

Your F/A-18A has a top speed of Mach 1.8 at a maximum altitude of 50,000 feet.

The afterburner, Radar System Display, and Weapon Tracking Indicator may be used during this scenario.

Your only armament is one 20mm M61A1 cannon with 500 rounds of ammunition mounted in the jet's nose and six AGM-88 HARM ASMs carried on external stores.

Mission Objectives. Supress all SAM sites.

Flying the Mission.

Step 1. Take off from the aircraft carrier *USS Coral Sea*.

Step 2. Never exceed an indicated airspeed of Mach 1.8 or an altitude of 50,000 feet.

Step 3. Climb to an altitude of 5,000 feet.

Step 4. Locate the Benghazi area on your radar.

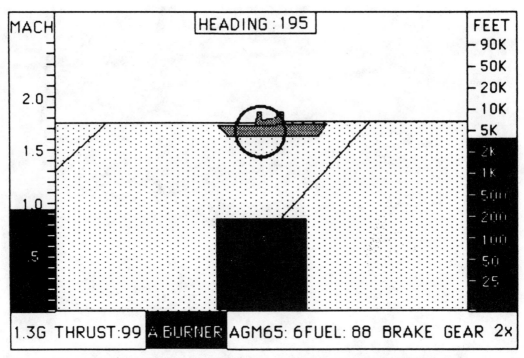

MACH | HEADING:195 | FEET

2.0

1.5

1.0

.5

90K
50K
20K
10K
5K
2K
1K
500
200
100
50
25

1.3G THRUST:99 A.BURNER AGM65: 6 FUEL: 88 BRAKE GEAR 2x

Fig. 8-1. An overly aggressive Libyan cruiser makes a nice target for this closing F/A-18A.

Step 5. Attack any SAM site that fires on you (Fig. 8-1). Evade all enemy SAM fire.
Step 6. Return to *USS Coral Sea* and land.
Mission Debriefing. You will have successfully flown this mission if you:

☐ Stayed within the performance boundaries of the F/A-18A.
☐ Located and destroyed all active SAM sites.
☐ Safely completed the mission.

50. TARGET TRIPOLI

Simultaneously with the U.S. Navy's air strike on Benghazi, 18 General Dynamics F-111Fs from various air bases located in Great Britain bombed three targets in Tripoli, Libya. The Al Azziziyah barracks, Sidi Bilal port facilities, and Tripoli Airport were all hit by the variable-geometry winged strike fighter/bombers. Using Paveway 2 500- and 2,000lb bombs under the guidance of the Pave Tack target-acquisition system, all of the targets were struck, although the final damage was slight. Whereas the Navy's bombing was deemed successful, the Air Force's effort was hampered by three significant events. First, France refused to allow the F-111Fs passage through their airspace, which lengthened the flight by a factor of two. Second, five of the F-111Fs were unable to locate their targets and failed to drop any ordinance. Lastly, one of the F-111Fs was lost, apparently shot down by Libyan SAMs.

Fig. 8-2. A heavily laden FB-111A uses its afterburners during this takeoff.

Mission Setup.
Select Game Mode.
Press 2.
Choose Skill Level.
Press 1.
Select Aircraft Type.
Press 2.
Select Armament.
Press 3 three times. Total 0.
Press 4 two times. Total 6.
Press 5.
Your F-111F has a top speed of Mach 1.9 at a maximum altitude of 60,000 feet.
The afterburner, Radar System Display, and Weapon Tracking Indicator may be used during this scenario.
Your only armament is six 500lb Paveway 2 bombs carried on external stores.
Mission Objectives. Bomb the Al Azziziyah barracks.
Flying the Mission.
Step 1. Take off from runway 4L (Fig. 8-2).
Step 2. Never exceed an indicated airspeed of Mach 1.9 or an altitude of 60,000 feet.

118

Step 3. Climb to an altitude of 500 feet.

Step 4. Activate the M61A1 Weapon System. Fire off all 500 rounds of your cannon ammunition. You will have 0 rounds of ammunition for combat.

Step 5. Locate the barracks on your radar.

Step 6. Approach the target low and slow (use an indicated airspeed of approximately Mach .5). Make your bombing run. Evade all enemy SAM fire.

Step 7. Return to the home base and land.

Step 8. Taxi into the hangar.

Mission Debriefing. You will have successfully flown this mission if you:

- ☐ Stayed within the performance boundaries of the F-111F.
- ☐ Located and destroyed the barracks from an altitude of 500 feet.
- ☐ Safely completed the mission. Any mission that is conducted at a low altitude is prone to heavy SAM fire. This point is reinforced by the loss of one F-111F during the 15 April 1986 raid.

Chapter 9

High-Speed Aerobatics

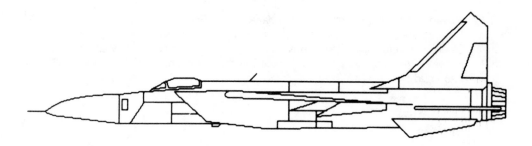

51. LADIES AND GENTLEMEN, THE THUNDERBIRDS

With the arrival of jet aircraft, an old thrill was revived. Crowd-pleasing aerobatics performed at high speeds added a new element of excitement similar to that which had sparked the barnstormers of the 1920s. Daring death and winning became the hallmark of the jet aerobatic team. In 1953, the U.S. Air Force fielded a team of experienced pilots for flying F-84Gs in special aerial demonstrations. The Thunderbirds had been born (Fig. 55-1). Usually flying the most sophisticated aircraft in the Air Force's current inventory, the Thunderbirds adopted the F-16A for its 1983 performance schedule. This switch to Fighting Falcons is an important mark in the short life of the Thunderbirds. No other aerobatic team in the world flies as sophisticated an aircraft as the F-16A. In fact, with their current steed, the Thunderbirds have become the premier aerobatic team in the history of aviation.

Mission Setup.
Select Game Mode.
Press 3.
Choose Skill Level.
Press 1.
Select Aircraft Type.
Press 2.

Your F-16A has a top speed of Mach 2 at a maximum altitude of 60,000 feet.

The afterburner, Radar System Display, and Weapon Tracking Indicator may be used during this scenario.

Optional subLOGIC Scenery Disks can be used for background during this scenario. The lack of an accurate Fuel Quantity Indicator limits the realism with the Scenery Disks, however.

Mission Objectives. Fly a series of Thunderbird aerobatic maneuvers (Fig. 9-2).
Flying the Mission.
Note: Fly this entire scenario from the Control Tower Mode viewpoint.

Fig. 9-1. In the late 1960s and early 1970s, the Thunderbirds flew F-4Es in tight, high-speed formations.

Step 1. Take off from runway 0.

Step 2. Never exceed an indicated airspeed of Mach 1 or an altitude of 15,000 feet.

Step 3. Climb to an altitude of 50 feet.

Step 4. Pitch the aircraft up 90 degrees at the end of the runway (Fig. 9-3).

Step 5. Rotate over and perform an Immelmann at 10,000 feet.

Step 6. Approach the middle of the runway at 250 feet and perform rolls down the length of the runway.

Step 7. Fly directly at the control tower on a heading of 270 degrees at 250 feet and make a 90 degree bank to the right when over runway 0.

Step 8. Increase your throttle and engage the afterburner. Make a high-speed pass at an altitude of 500 feet directly down runway 0 on a heading of 0 degrees. Avoid breaking Mach 1 in this maneuver. You might need to use the speed brake to keep this from happening.

Step 9. Perform a slow loop on a heading of 0 degrees starting at an altitude of 500 feet.

Step 10. Execute a slow loop plus rolls on a heading of 180 degrees starting at an altitude of 500 feet.

Step 11. End the demonstration with a high show bomb burst.

Step 12. On a heading of 180 degrees, pitch up for a maximum bank landing midway down runway 18.

Step 13. Land on runway 0.

Step 14. Taxi into the hangar.

Mission Debriefing. You will have successfully flown this mission if you:

☐ Stayed within the performance boundaries of the F-16A.
☐ Performed all of the maneuvers from the Control Tower Mode viewpoint at the set altitudes. Flying this scenario with a Scenery Disk will alter many of the fixed indicator readings.
☐ Safely completed the mission.

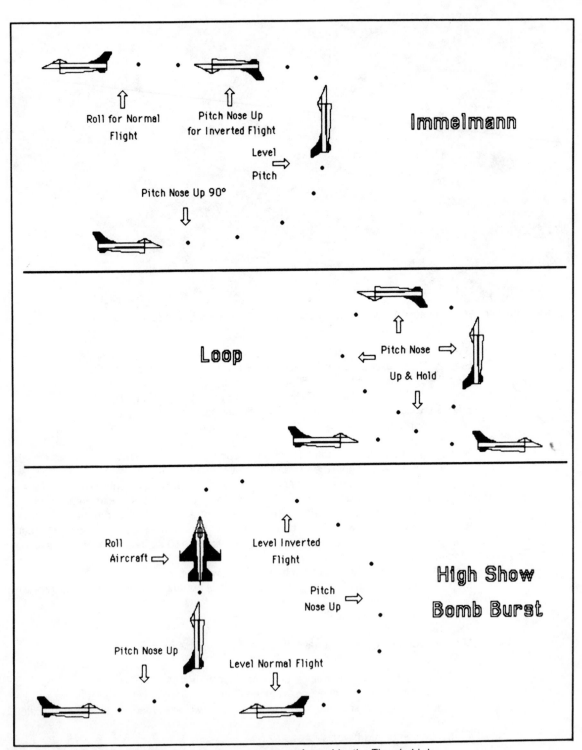

Fig. 9-2. Three of the more difficult aerobatic maneuvers performed by the Thunderbirds.

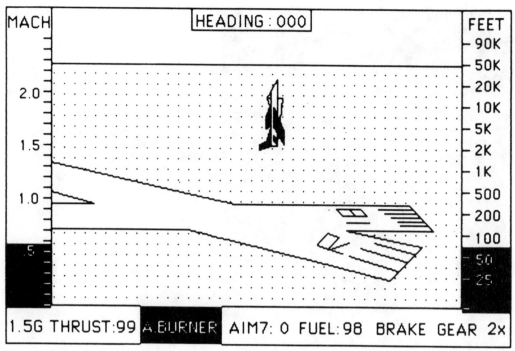

MACH | HEADING: 000 | FEET
2.0
1.5
1.0
.5

90K
50K
20K
10K
5K
2K
1K
500
200
100
50
25

1.5G THRUST:99 A.BURNER AIM7: 0 FUEL:98 BRAKE GEAR 2x

Fig. 9-3. Flying the Thunderbird performance from the control tower viewpoint will be one of the toughest challenges faced by the JET pilot.

52. PRESENTING THE BLUE ANGELS

In an effort to display precision flying techniques, the U.S. Navy organized a special Flight Demonstration Squadron in early 1946. Later that same year, this squadron, now called the Blue Angels, gave their first public performance on 15 June. Flying Grumman F6F Hellcat piston-powered aircraft, veteran World War II naval pilots executed several in-flight maneuvers from a tight diamond formation. As advances in aviation technology reached the U.S. Navy's inventory, the Blue Angels adopted the new aircraft for their flight demonstrations. This included a switch to the F9F-2 Panther in 1949. An interesting footnote to the use of the Panther is that the Blue Angels became a combat squadron during the Korean War aboard USS Princeton—a noteworthy first for an aerobatic team. In 1974, the modern Blue Angels emerged (see Fig. 9-4). Now the modest A-4F Skyhawk II became their main performance aircraft, replacing the spectacular F-4J Phantom II.

Mission Setup.
Select Game Mode.
Press 3.
Choose Skill Level.
Press 1.
Select Aircraft Type.
Press 1.
Your A-4F has a top speed of Mach .9 at a maximum altitude of 49,000 feet.
The Radar System Display and Weapon Tracking Indicator may be used during this scenario. The afterburner may not be used.
Optional subLOGIC Scenery Disks can be used for background during this scenario. The

Fig. 9-4. An inverted high show bomb burst is one of several twists used by the Blue Angels during their aerobatic demonstration.

lack of an accurate Fuel Quantity Indicator limits the realism with the Scenery Disks, however.

Mission Objectives. Fly a series of Blue Angel aerobatic maneuvers.

Flying the Mission.

Note: Fly this entire scenario from the Control Tower Mode viewpoint.

Step 1. Take off from the aircraft carrier.

Step 2. Never exceed an indicated airspeed of Mach 1 or an altitude of 15,000 feet.

Step 3. Climb to an altitude of 50 feet.

Step 4. Pitch the aircraft up 90 degrees off the bow of the carrier.

Step 5. Rotate over and perform an Immelmann at 10,000 feet.

Step 6. Fly directly at the control tower on a heading of 180 degrees at 250 feet and make a 90 degree bank to the right when over carrier's deck.

Step 7. Fly down the middle of the carrier's deck at an altitude of 250 feet and perform four rolls down the length of the deck.

Step 8. Increase your throttle to 99 percent. Make a high-speed pass at an altitude of 500 feet directly down the deck from stem to stern on a heading of 270 degrees. Avoid breaking Mach 1 in this maneuver. You might need to use the speed brake to keep this from happening.

Step 9. Perform a slow loop on a heading of 90 degrees, starting at an altitude of 500 feet.

Step 10. Execute a slow loop plus rolls on a heading of 270 degrees, starting at an altitude of 500 feet.

Step 11. Line up with the stern of the ship. As you pass over the stern, pitch the aircraft to 45 degrees, perform a series of left rolls, and end with a 90 degree bank to the right.

Step 12. End the performance with a high show bomb burst.

Step 13. On a heading of 90 degrees, pitch up for a maximum bank landing on the carrier's deck.

Step 14. Land on the carrier and engage the arresting cable.

Mission Debriefing. You will have successfully flown this mission if you:

☐ Stayed within the performance boundaries of the A-4F.
☐ Performed all of the maneuvers from the Control Tower Mode viewpoint at the set altitudes. Flying this scenario with a Scenery Disk will alter many of the fixed indicator readings.
☐ Safely completed the mission.

Chapter 10

Foreign Aerial Engagements

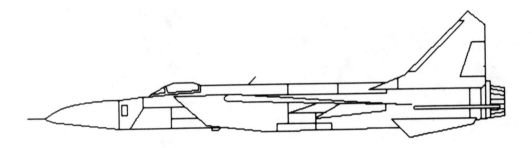

53. GULF WAR

When the Shah of Iran left his country in February 1979, neighboring Iraq saw this revolution as an opportunity to secure its position in the Persian Gulf. In 1980, Iraq struck at the Iranian oil complex at Abadan. Meanwhile, the Revolutionary Council in Tehran declared war on Iraq. Thus the Persian Gulf was ignited in a bitter war for the control of the vast oilfields surrounding the region. Virtually any shipping entering the waters of the Persian Gulf had become a surface target for the ranging air forces of both Iran and Iraq. On 12 August 1986, Iraqi Dassault-Breguet Mirage F1.Cs staged the first long-range raid against Iranian shipping at the Sirri Island terminal. One tanker was sunk and two others were heavily damaged.

Mission Setup.
Select Game Mode.
Press 2.
Choose Skill Level.
Press 1.
Select Aircraft Type.
Press 1.
Select Armament.
Press 3 four times. Total 1.
Press 4 three times. Total 0.
Press 5.
Your Mirage F1.C has a top speed of Mach 1.8 at a maximum altitude of 60,000 feet.
The afterburner, Radar System Display, and Weapon Tracking Indicator may be used during this scenario.
Your only armament is two 30mm DEFA 553 cannons with 200 rounds of ammunition mounted in the jet's nose and 1 AS.37 Martel ARM carried on external stores.
Mission Objectives. Sink the tanker *Azarpad*.

Flying the Mission.
Step 1. Take off from the aircraft carrier.
Step 2. Never exceed an indicated airspeed of Mach 1.8 or an altitude of 60,000 feet.
Step 3. Climb to an altitude of 20,000 feet.
Step 4. Activate the M61A1 Weapon System. Fire off 300 rounds of your ammunition. You now have 200 rounds of cannon ammunition for combat.
Step 5. Locate the target on your radar.
Step 6. Make your bombing run. Evade all enemy SAM fire.
Step 7. Return to the carrier and land.
Mission Debriefing. You will have successfully flown this mission if you:

☐ Stayed within the performance boundaries of the Mirage F1.C.
☐ Sank the Iranian tanker Azarpad.
☐ Safely completed the mission.

54. BLACK BUCK

Looking for a war, Argentina invaded a small island chain in the South Atlantic on 2 April 1982. The only trouble with this plan was that the Falkland Islands belonged to the United Kingdom. Based on this senseless aggression, Britain declared war on Argentina and launched a carrier task force to the South Atlantic. Thinking that any British action would take four weeks to reach them, the Argentines slowly prepared their forces for a battle that was one month away. England had other ideas, however. Using long-range Hawker Siddeley Vulcan B. Mk. 2 bombers, No. 44 Squadron conducted operation Black Buck. Flying at low-altitude, a solitary Vulcan B. Mk. 2 bombed the airfield at Port Stanley on 1 May 1982. Of the 14 bombs dropped, only one made a hit on the runway.
Mission Setup.
Select Game Mode.
Press 2.
Choose Skill Level.
Press 0.
Select Aircraft Type.
Press 2.
Select Armament.
Press 3 three times. Total 0.
Press 4 two times. Total 6.
Press 5.
Your Vulcan B. Mk. 2 has a top speed of Mach .8 at a maximum altitude of 65,000 feet. The Radar System Display and Weapon Tracking Indicator may be used during this scenario. The afterburner may not be used in this scenario.
Your only armament is six 1000lb bombs carried in the internal bomb bay.
Mission Objectives. Bomb the Port Stanley airfield.
Flying the Mission.
Step 1. Take off from runway 0.
Step 2. Never exceed an indicated airspeed of Mach .8 or an altitude of 65,000 feet.
Step 3. Climb to an altitude of 1000 feet.

Step 4. Activate the M61A1 Weapon System. Fire off all 500 rounds of your cannon ammunition. You will have 0 rounds of ammunition for combat.

Step 5. Locate the airfield on your radar.

Step 6. Approach the target low and slow (use an indicated airspeed of approximately Mach .5). Make your bombing run.

Step 7. Return to the home base and land.

Step 8. Taxi into the hangar.

Mission Debriefing. You will have successfully flown this mission if you:

☐ Stayed within the performance boundaries of the Vulcan B. Mk. 2.

☐ Located and destroyed the Port Stanley airfield from an altitude of 1000 feet.

☐ Safely completed the mission.

55. AIR COMBAT OVER THE FALKLAND ISLANDS

Once the British task force arrived in the vicinity of the Falkland Islands, air superiority became a prime concern. A land-based, jet-equipped air force would have easy hunting with the British fleet floating several miles off the coast. Therefore, British Aerospace Sea Harrier FRS.Mk 1s were flown in pairs as a part of the air defense of the fleet. The Sea Harriers proved quite capable of handling the Argentine A-4Qs and Mirage IIIs. The Sea Harrier force did suffer casualties at the hand of the Argentine SAM and ground fire. If nothing else, the Falkland Island campaign proved that a sea-based air force can prevent the destruction of a fleet through tactical air defense.

Mission Setup.

Select Game Mode.

Press 1.

Choose Skill Level.

Press 2.

Select Aircraft Type.

Press 1.

Select Armament.

Press 1 zero times. Total 4.

Press 2 three times. Total 0.

Press 5.

Your Sea Harrier has a top speed of Mach .9 at a maximum altitude of 50,000 feet.

The Radar System Display and Weapon Tracking Indicator may be used during this scenario.

The afterburner may not be used on the Sea Harrier.

Your only armament is four AIM-9L Sidewinder AAMs carried on external stores.

Mission Objectives. Defend the British fleet from enemy jets.

Flying the Mission.

Step 1. Take off from the aircraft carrier.

Step 2. Never exceed an indicated airspeed of Mach .9 or an altitude of 50,000 feet.

Step 3. Climb to an altitude of 5,000 feet.

Step 4. Activate the M61A1 Weapon System. Fire off 500 rounds of your ammunition. You will have 0 rounds of cannon ammunition for combat.

Step 5. Locate enemy jets on your radar.

Step 6. Shoot down any aircraft that attempt to attack either you or the task force. Evade all enemy missile fire.

Step 7. Return to the carrier and land.

Mission Debriefing. You will have successfully flown this mission if you:

☐ Stayed within the performance boundaries of the Sea Harrier.
☐ Shot down any enemy aircraft.
☐ Safely completed the mission.

56. NATO AIR SUPERIORITY

Should a war ever rage through Europe again, air superiority will be the key to success. Today's frontline air superiority fighter is the F-16A. Equipped with two AIM-9L Sidewinder AAMs, the F-16A is able to travel 445 nautical miles and engage in aerial combat for 15 minutes (Fig. 10-1). This would extend the NATO range of air superiority well into the Warsaw Pact countries.

Mission Setup.
Select Game Mode.
Press 1.
Choose Skill Level.
Press 7.

Fig. 10-1. Four F-16As each armed with two AIM-9L AAMs fly in a tight patrol formation. This formation would not be used during a combat air superiority mission. (courtesy General Dynamics Corp.)

Select Aircraft Type.

Press 2.

Select Armament.

Press 1 five times. Total 2.

Press 2 three times. Total 0.

Press 5.

Your F-16A has a top speed of Mach 2 at a maximum altitude of 60,000 feet.

The afterburner, Radar System Display, and Weapon Tracking Indicator may be used during this scenario.

Your armament is one 20mm M61A1 cannon with 500 rounds of ammunition mounted in the jet's nose and two AIM-9L Sidewinder AAMs carried on external stores.

Mission Objectives. Achieve air superiority over Europe.

Flying the Mission.

Step 1. Take off from runway 0.

Step 2. Never exceed an indicated airspeed of Mach 2 or an altitude of 60,000 feet.

Step 3. Climb to an altitude of 30,000 feet.

Step 4. Locate enemy aircraft on your radar.

Step 5. Shoot down the enemy jets. Evade all enemy missile fire.

Step 6. Return to the home base and land.

Step 7. Taxi into the hangar.

Mission Debriefing. You will have successfully flown this mission if you:

☐ Stayed within the performance boundaries of the F-16A.

☐ Acquired air superiority over the NATO conflict area.

☐ Safely completed the mission.

57. NATO CLOSE AIR SUPPORT

Any success at halting a Communist advance through Europe will depend heavily on the F-16A's ability to provide close air support for NATO ground forces. Forward air controllers will direct the NATO jets to specific targets. Once the jets are in the vicinity, they will need to use precision bombing techniques for neutralizing the target. The heavy presence of Soviet SAMs will make European close air support an extremely difficult mission.

Mission Setup.

Select Game Mode.

Press 2.

Choose Skill Level.

Press 8.

Select Aircraft Type.

Press 2.

Select Armament.

Press 3 three times. Total 0.

Press 4 two times. Total 6.

Press 5.

Your F-16A has a top speed of Mach 2 at a maximum altitude of 60,000 feet.

The afterburner, Radar System Display, and Weapon Tracking Indicator may be used during this scenario.

Fig. 10-2. Following a low-altitude pass, this A-10A begins to bank left in a tight turn.

Your only armament is one 20mm M61A1 cannon with 500 rounds of ammunition mounted in the jet's nose and six MK-82 500lb bombs carried on external stores.

Mission Objectives. Lend close air support to NATO forces.

Flying the Mission.

Step 1. Take off from runway 0.

Step 2. Never exceed an indicated airspeed of Mach 2 or an altitude of 60,000 feet.

Step 3. Climb to an altitude of 10,000 feet.

Step 4. Locate the ground target on your radar.

Step 5. Make your bombing run. Evade all enemy SAM fire.

Step 7. Return to the home base and land.

Step 8. Taxi into the hangar.

Mission Debriefing. You will have successfully flown this mission if you:

☐ Stayed within the performance boundaries of the F-16A.

☐ Provided close air support.

☐ Safely completed the mission.

58. NATO LOW-LEVEL STRIKE

A unique aircraft will be used by NATO forces for low-level air strikes. The Fairchild A-10A Thunderbolt II is a potent strike aircraft that can carry a 16,000 pound offensive payload over a 285 mile operational radius (Fig. 10-2). Designed for low-speed flight, the A-10A answers many of the questions that were raised about the effectiveness of high-speed jet strike aircraft during the Vietnam War. The need for a strong low-level strike aircraft is especially important in Europe, where the Soviets have a distinct armor advantage. Therefore, the A-10A/AGM-65 combination is sometimes called the "Tank Killer."

Mission Setup.
Select Game Mode.
Press 2.
Choose Skill Level.
Press 2.
Select Aircraft Type.
Press 2.
Select Armament.
Press 3 two times. Total 6.
Press 4 two times. Total 6.
Press 5.
Your A-10A has a top speed of Mach .5 at a maximum altitude of 40,000 feet.
The Radar System Display and Weapon Tracking Indicator may be used during this scenario.
The afterburner may not be used during this scenario.
Your armament is one 30mm GAU-8/A cannon with 500 rounds of ammunition mounted in the jet's nose and six MK-82 500lb bombs and six AGM-65D Maverick ASMs carried on external stores.

Mission Objectives. Level ground targets in eastern Europe.

Flying the Mission.
Step 1. Take off from runway 0.
Step 2. Never exceed an indicated airspeed of Mach .5 or an altitude of 40,000 feet.
Step 3. Climb to an altitude of 1,000 feet.
Step 4. Locate the ground target on your radar.
Step 5. Make your bombing run. Evade all enemy SAM fire.
Step 6. Destroy any other targets that present themselves.
Step 7. Return to the home base and land.
Step 8. Taxi into the hangar.

Mission Debriefing. You will have successfully flown this mission if you:

☐ Stayed within the performance boundaries of the A-10A.
☐ Located and destroyed all ground targets.
☐ Safely completed the mission.

59. NATO EXTENSIVE STRIKE

Containment will be important in halting any Soviet drive through western Europe. Should a break-out occur, however, a quick and extensive air strike will be the only means for thwarting the total collapse of Europe. F-16As equipped with 2,000lb MK-84 bombs will be able to fly numerous lightning strikes against the massing Soviet troop concentrations.

Mission Setup.
Select Game Mode.
Press 2.
Choose Skill Level.
Press 2.
Select Aircraft Type.
Press 2.

Select Armament.
Press 3 three times. Total 0.
Press 4 five times. Total 2.
Press 5.
Your F-16A has a top speed of Mach 2 at a maximum altitude of 60,000 feet.
The afterburner, Radar System Display, and Weapon Tracking Indicator may be used during this scenario.
Your armament is one 20mm M61A1 cannon with 500 rounds of ammunition mounted in the jet's nose and two MK-84 2,000lb bombs carried on external stores.
Mission Objectives. Contain a Soviet breakout.
Flying the Mission.
Step 1. Take off from runway 0.
Step 2. Never exceed an indicated airspeed of Mach 2 or an altitude of 60,000 feet.
Step 3. Climb to an altitude of 30,000 feet.
Step 4. Locate the target on your radar.
Step 5. Dive to 500 feet and make your bombing run. Evade all enemy SAM fire.
Step 6. Return to the home base and land.
Step 7. Taxi into the hangar.
Mission Debriefing. You will have successfully flown this mission if you:

☐ Stayed within the performance boundaries of the F-16A.
☐ Halted the Soviet drive.
☐ Safely completed the mission.

60. NATO SEA LANE INTERDICTION

Around Europe the seas belong to NATO—that is, unless a Soviet submarine squadron appears. This threat has been tested with a large degree of success by Soviet submarines probing Sweden's territorial waters. By using F-16As loaded with AGM-84 Harpoons, NATO forces will be able to control the surface vessel traffic throughout the North Atlantic. While this doesn't eliminate the submarine threat, it does restrict the remainder of the Soviet's surface fleet.
Mission Setup.
Select Game Mode.
Press 2.
Choose Skill Level.
Press 3.
Select Aircraft Type.
Press 1.
Select Armament.
Press 3 five times. Total 2.
Press 4 three times. Total 0.
Press 5.
Your F-16A has a top speed of Mach 2 at a maximum altitude of 60,000 feet.
The afterburner, Radar System Display, and Weapon Tracking Indicator may be used during this scenario.
Your armament is one 20mm M61A1 cannon with 500 rounds of ammunition mounted in

the jet's nose and two AGM-84A Harpoon ASMs carried on external stores.

Mission Objectives. Sink all Soviet surface vessels.

Flying the Mission.

Step 1. Take off from the aircraft carrier.

Step 2. Never exceed an indicated airspeed of Mach 2 or an altitude of 60,000 feet.

Step 3. Climb to an altitude of 20,000 feet.

Step 4. Locate the Soviet target on your radar.

Step 5. Attack and sink the vessel. Evade all enemy SAM fire.

Step 6. Return to the carrier and land.

Mission Debriefing. You will have successfully flown this mission if you:

☐ Stayed within the performance boundaries of the F-16A.

☐ Sank any encountered Soviet shipping.

☐ Safely completed the mission.

61. NATO HIGH-PERFORMANCE INTERCEPTION

The presence of high-performance Soviet fighters has placed yet another role onto the shoulders of the F-16A. Even with advanced radar warning systems, Soviet aircraft can be over NATO airfields in less than 15 minutes. This dictates a high-performance interception mission for the F-16As, which would prevent the Soviet violation of NATO's airspace. Of course, the degree of speed and altitude required by this mission reduces the F-16A's effective range to under 370 nautical miles.

Mission Setup.

Select Game Mode.

Press 1.

Choose Skill Level.

Press 8.

Select Aircraft Type.

Press 2.

Select Armament.

Press 1 five times. Total 2.

Press 2 three times. Total 0.

Press 5.

Your F-16A has a top speed of Mach 2 at a maximum altitude of 60,000 feet.

The afterburner, Radar System Display, and Weapon Tracking Indicator may be used during this scenario.

Your armament is one 20mm M61A1 cannon with 500 rounds of ammunition mounted in the jet's nose and two AIM-9L Sidewinder AAMs carried on external stores.

Mission Objectives. Engage enemy jets prior to their reaching NATO territory.

Flying the Mission.

Step 1. Take off from runway 0. Use a maximum power climb at Mach 1.5. Level at 20,000 feet and continue to accelerate.

Step 2. Never exceed an indicated airspeed of Mach 2 or an altitude of 60,000 feet.

Step 3. Climb to an altitude of 50,000 feet. Keep your indicated airspeed as high as possible.

Step 4. Locate enemy aircraft on your radar.

Step 5. Engage and shoot down the enemy jets. Evade all enemy missile fire.

Step 6. Mind your fuel consumption rate.

Step 7. Return to the home base and land.

Step 8. Taxi into the hangar.

Mission Debriefing. You will have successfully flown this mission if you:

☐ Stayed within the performance boundaries of the F-16A.

☐ Prevented the enemy jets from violating NATO airspace.

☐ Safely completed the mission.

62. BATTLE FOR THE MIDDLE EAST

Israel's presence in the Middle East has been a continual source of aggravation for its Arab neighbors. This hostile tension has forced Israel into a constant state of military upgrade. As the Arab countries with a Soviet alliance acquire the newer MiGs, Israel is in turn obligated to purchase more modern free world aircraft. This dependence on an outside source forced Israel to begin its own campaign at designing "home-built" aircraft. One result from this program is the Israel Aircraft Industries' Lavi Fighter. The Lavi uses the same basic airframe as the F-16A. Israel hopes that the survivability of the Lavi will make it capable of meeting future MiG threats.

Mission Setup.

Select Game Mode.

Press 1.

Choose Skill Level.

Press 9.

Select Aircraft Type.

Press 2.

Select Armament.

Press 1 five times. Total 2.

Press 2 five times. Total 2.

Press 5.

Your Lavi has a top speed of Mach 2 at a maximum altitude of 60,000 feet.

The afterburner, Radar System Display, and Weapon Tracking Indicator may be used during this scenario.

Your armament is one 20mm M61A1 cannon with 500 rounds of ammunition mounted in the jet's nose and two AIM-9L Sidewinder and two Rafael Python AAMs carried on external stores.

Mission Objectives. Meet MiG-29 Fulcrums over Syria.

Flying the Mission.

Step 1. Take off from runway 0.

Step 2. Never exceed an indicated airspeed of Mach 2 or an altitude of 60,000 feet.

Step 3. Climb to an altitude of 30,000 feet.

Step 4. Locate enemy aircraft on your radar.

Step 5. Engage and shoot down the enemy jets. Evade all enemy missile fire. The MiG-29 is a highly maneuverable air superiority fighter. Its AAMs have a good range and are accurate.

Step 6. Mind your fuel consumption rate.

Step 7. Return to the home base and land.

Step 8. Taxi into the hangar.

Mission Debriefing. You will have successfully flown this mission if you:

☐ Stayed within the performance boundaries of the Lavi.
☐ Engaged and shot down a MiG-29.
☐ Safely completed the mission.

Chapter 11

Top Gun

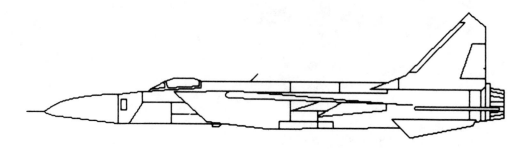

63.   MIRAMAR AIR DUEL

Dogfighting in jets has been difficult for American pilots in the past. Following the terrific kill ratio of the Korean War, the enemy's skill has increased while that of the United States has remained fixed at a wholly inadequate level. In an effort to halt this stagnation, the U.S. Navy started a Navy Fighter Weapons School at Miramar Naval Air Station in 1968 (*note*: this program has a counterpart in the Air Force's Dissimilar Air Combat Tactics school at Nellis AFB). Nicknamed "Top Gun," the first graduates from Miramar were able to put their skills to the test during Operation Linebacker over North Vietnam. At Top Gun, the motto is: "You fight like you train."

Mission Setup.
Select Game Mode.
Press 1.
Choose Skill Level.
Press 4.
Select Aircraft Type.
Press 1.
Select Armament.
Press 1 five times. Total 2.
Press 2 five times. Total 2.
Press 5.

Your F-14A has a top speed of Mach 2.1 at a maximum altitude of 56,000 feet.

The afterburner, Radar System Display, and Weapon Tracking Indicator may be used during this scenario.

Your armament is one 20mm M61A1 cannon with 500 rounds of ammunition mounted in the jet's nose and two AIM-9L Sidewinder and two AIM-54A Phoenix AAMs carried on external stores.

Mission Objectives. Become a Top Gun.

Fig. 11-1. Taking off with extended wings and engaged afterburners, this F-14A sports an impressive list of performance features.

Flying the Mission.
Step 1. Take off from the aircraft carrier.
Step 2. Never exceed an indicated airspeed of Mach 2.1 or an altitude of 56,000 feet.
Step 3. Climb to an altitude of 5,000 feet (Fig. 11-1).
Step 4. Locate the enemy aircraft on your radar.
Step 5. Engage and shoot down the enemy jets. Evade all enemy missile fire. Fix your ceiling at 5,000 feet. Try to stay within an altitude of 500-1,000 feet.
Step 6. Mind your fuel consumption rate.
Step 7. Return to the carrier and land.
Mission Debriefing. You will have successfully flown this mission if you:

☐ Stayed within the performance boundaries of the F-14A.
☐ Shot down the aggressor aircraft.
☐ Safely completed the mission.

64. OPERATION GREEN FLAG

The McDonnell Douglas F/A-18A Hornet operates as a joint service fighter/bomber. Both U.S. Navy and U.S. Marine squadrons have now been equipped with this problem-plagued aircraft. What started as a naval call for a carrier-based aircraft with capabilities equal to the F-16A ended as the dual role F/A-18A. Capable of air superiority as well as ground strike missions, the Hornet has fallen into disfavor with its pilots due to landing gear failures and performance faults.
Mission Setup.
Select Game Mode.
Press 2.
Choose Skill Level.
Press 6.
Select Aircraft Type.

Press 1.

Select Armament.

Press 3 zero times. Total 4.

Press 4 three times. Total 0.

Press 5.

Your F/A-18A has a top speed of Mach 1.8 at a maximum altitude of 60,000 feet.

The afterburner, Radar System Display, and Weapon Tracking Indicator may be used during this scenario.

Your armament is one 20mm M61A1 cannon with 500 rounds of ammunition mounted in the jet's nose and four AGM-65E Maverick ASMs carried on external stores.

Mission Objectives. Sink the target practice surface vessels.

Flying the Mission.

Step 1. Take off from the aircraft carrier.

Step 2. Never exceed an indicated airspeed of Mach 1.8 or an altitude of 60,000 feet.

Step 3. Climb to an altitude of 15,000 feet.

Step 4. Locate the practice target on your radar.

Step 5. Attack and sink the vessel. Evade all enemy SAM fire.

Step 6. Return to the carrier and land.

Mission Debriefing. You will have successfully flown this mission if you:

☐ Stayed within the performance boundaries of the F/A-18A.
☐ Sank the target vessel.
☐ Safely completed the mission.

65. THE *WESTERN SUN* ACCIDENT

The crew of the *Western Sun* oil tanker thought that World War III had erupted on 1 August 1986 when an unarmed missile hit their ship. Sailing off the coast of Virginia, the *Western Sun* was 30 miles from a known U.S. Navy weapons testing range. Somewhere over the test range, an F-14A from VF-74 based at Oceana NAS in Virginia Beach accidentally fired one of its missiles. The missile found its way to the *Western Sun* and dug a 2.5 foot hole in its superstructure. Luckily, the missile was inert and no one was seriously injured. The final score was: Navy 1, Commercial Shipping 0.

Mission Setup.

Select Game Mode.

Press 2.

Choose Skill Level.

Press 0.

Select Aircraft Type.

Press 1.

Select Armament.

Press 3 five times. Total 2.

Press 4 three times. Total 0.

Press 5.

Your F-14A has a top speed of Mach 2.1 at a maximum altitude of 56,000 feet.

The afterburner, Radar System Display, and Weapon Tracking Indicator may be used during this scenario.

Your armament is ridiculously overmatched for your opponent.

Mission Objectives. Punch a hole in the *Western Sun*.

Flying the Mission.

Step 1. Take off from the aircraft carrier.

Step 2. Never exceed an indicated airspeed of Mach 2.1 or an altitude of 56,000 feet.

Step 3. Climb to an altitude of 1,000 feet.

Step 4. Locate the *Western Sun* on your radar.

Step 5. Fire one of your ASMs.

Step 6. Hit the *Western Sun* with the missile.

Step 7. Return to the carrier and land.

Mission Debriefing. You will have successfully flown this mission if you:

☐ Stayed within the performance boundaries of the F-14A.

☐ Scared the heck out of the crew of the *Western Sun*.

☐ Safely completed the mission to face disciplinary action.

66. RIMPAC 86

Numerous naval exercises are conducted on a yearly basis as a means of testing the readiness of the U.S. fleet. Occasionally, these exercises develop a new tactic that will be adopted in the naval combat doctrine. One such tactic was tested during the Navy's maneuvers of RIMPAC 86. By using EMCON (EMission CONtrol) measures, special aerial launch procedures, and weather coverage, the aircraft carrier *USS Ranger* "disappeared" off the face of the Pacific ocean. Essentially, all of these techniques contribute to disguising the appearance of an aircraft carrier on radar scopes. The proven nature of hiding an aircraft carrier was actually tested under combat conditions one month prior to "losing" *USS Ranger*. During the bombing of Benghazi, *USS Coral Sea* and *USS America* were both lost until the moment of the attack.

Mission Setup.

Select Game Mode.

Press 1.

Choose Skill Level.

Press 7.

Select Aircraft Type.

Press 1.

Select Armament.

Press 1 zero times. Total 4.

Press 2 five times. Total 2.

Press 5.

Your F/A-18A has a top speed of Mach 1.8 at a maximum altitude of 60,000 feet.

The afterburner, Radar System Display, and Weapon Tracking Indicator may be used during this scenario.

Your armament is one 20mm M61A1 cannon with 500 rounds of ammunition mounted in the jet's nose and four AIM-9L Sidewinder and two AIM-54A Phoenix AAMs carried on external stores.

Mission Objectives. Use aircraft carrier hiding techniques to engage enemy fighters.

Flying the Mission.

Step 1. Take off from *USS Ranger*. Stay on the deck at a reduced airspeed. Take a heading of 4 degrees.

Step 2. Never exceed an indicated airspeed of Mach 1.8 or an altitude of 60,000 feet.

Step 3. Wait until you are six miles from the carrier, then quickly climb to an altitude of 20,000 feet.

Step 4. Locate the enemy aircraft on your radar.

Step 5. Attack and shoot down the jets. Evade all enemy missile fire.

Step 6. Return to the carrier by hitting the deck six miles north of the carrier and assume a standard landing pattern.

Step 7. Land on *USS Ranger*.

Mission Debriefing. You will have successfully flown this mission if you:

☐ Stayed within the performance boundaries of the F/A-18A.
☐ Masked the location of *USS Ranger*.
☐ Downed the enemy aircraft.
☐ Safely completed the mission.

67. CHINA LAKE

In November 1943, the Navy needed a special weapons testing range for experimenting with 3.5 inch rockets. The selected area was north of Edwards AFB in south-central California. Named China Lake Naval Weapons Center, this reservation today houses many sophisticated test sites for maintaining a high degree of systems effectiveness. For example, the Electronic Warfare Threat Enviornment Simulation (EWTES) facility, also known as Echo range, duplicates the Soviet naval search and SAM tracking radar systems. By flying simulated attacks against Echo range, U.S. Navy attack aircraft can perfect maneuvers for dealing with Soviet SAM sites.

Mission Setup.

Select Game Mode.

Press 2.

Choose Skill Level.

Press 7.

Select Aircraft Type.

Press 1.

Select Armament.

Press 3 zero times. Total 4.

Press 4 three times. Total 0.

Press 5.

Your F/A-18A has a top speed of Mach 1.8 at a maximum altitude of 60,000 feet.

The afterburner, Radar System Display, and Weapon Tracking Indicator may be used during this scenario.

Your armament is one 20mm M61A1 cannon with 500 rounds of ammunition mounted in the jet's nose and four AGM-65E Maverick ASMs carried on external stores.

Mission Objectives. Hit the Echo range simulated Soviet target.

Flying the Mission.

Step 1. Take off from the aircraft carrier.

Step 2. Never exceed an indicated airspeed of Mach 1.8 or an altitude of 60,000 feet.

Step 3. Climb to an altitude of 5,000 feet.
Step 4. Locate the practice target on your radar.
Step 5. Attack and "destroy" the vessel. Evade all enemy SAM fire.
Step 6. Return to the carrier and land.
Mission Debriefing. You will have successfully flown this mission if you:

☐ Stayed within the performance boundaries of the F/A-18A.
☐ Completed the Echo range test.
☐ Safely completed the mission.

68. MEETING MSIP

Keeping an aircraft like the F-16A up-to-date with recent advances in aviation could mean vast remodelings costing several times the original purchase price of the aircraft. Luckily, General Dynamics made provisions for accommodating system upgrades inexpensively into assembly line F-16s. The program, known as the Multinational Staged Improvement Program (MSIP), prepares F-16s on the assembly line for technology that will be developed within the life of the aircraft. Therefore, new engines and improved avionics can be "plugged" into the new F-16s following the construction of the stock aircraft.
    Mission Setup.
    Select Game Mode.
    Press 2.
    Choose Skill Level.
    Press 3.
    Select Aircraft Type.
    Press 2.
    Select Armament.
    Press 3 five times. Total 2.
    Press 4 three times. Total 0.
    Press 5.
    Your F-16A has a top speed of Mach 2 at a maximum altitude of 60,000 feet.
    The afterburner, Radar System Display, and Weapon tracking Indicator may be used during this scenario.
    Your armament is one 20mm M61A1 cannon with 500 rounds of ammunition mounted in the jet's nose and two Penguin ASMs carried on external stores.
    Mission Objectives. Conduct a land test of the Penguin ASM.
    Flying the Mission.
Step 1. Take off from runway 0.
Step 2. Never exceed an indicated airspeed of Mach 2 or an altitude of 60,000 feet.
Step 3. Climb to an altitude of 30,000 feet.
Step 4. Locate the target on your radar.
Step 5. Dive to 500 feet and make your bombing run. Evade all enemy SAM fire.
Step 6. Return to the home base and land.
Step 7. Taxi into the hangar.
    Mission Debriefing. You will have successfully flown this mission if you:

□ Stayed within the performance boundaries of the F-16A.
□ Successfully launched the two Penguin ASMs.
□ Safely completed the mission.

69. PACE EAGLE

The McDonnell-Douglas F-15A Eagle was originally designed as a "Foxbat Killer." The large presence of MiG-25 Foxbats in the Soviet air arsenal demanded a suitable U.S. air superiority fighter that could dogfight the Foxbat and win. Only by keeping abreast of current technology will the Eagle be able to retain its "Foxbat Killer" status. McDonnell Douglas' upgrade program is called Pace Eagle. Pace Eagle F-15s will sport new engines, advanced avionics, and improved weapon systems.

Mission Setup.

Select Game Mode.

Press 1.

Choose Skill Level.

Press 9.

Select Aircraft Type.

Press 2.

Select Armament.

Press 1 zero times. Total 4.

Press 2 five times. Total 2.

Press 5.

Your Pace Eagle has a top speed of Mach 2 at a maximum altitude of 60,000 feet.

The afterburner, Radar System Display, and Weapon Tracking Indicator may be used during this scenario.

Your armament is one 20mm M61A1 cannon with 500 rounds of ammunition mounted in the jet's nose and four AIM-9X Sidewinder and two AIM-7X Sparrow AAMs carried on external stores.

Mission Objectives. Test the new AMRAAM (Advanced Medium-Range Air-to-Air Missile) system.

Flying the Mission.

Step 1. Take off from runway 0.

Step 2. Never exceed an indicated airspeed of Mach 2 or an altitude of 60,000 feet.

Step 3. Climb to an altitude of 40,000 feet.

Step 4. Locate the target on your radar.

Step 5. Engage the target jets in combat.

Step 6. Return to the home base and land.

Step 7. Taxi into the hangar.

Mission Debriefing. You will have successfully flown this mission if you:

□ Stayed within the performance boundaries of the Pace Eagle.
□ Downed the target jets with the ARMAAM system.
□ Safely completed the mission.

70. ADVANCED HORNET

McDonnell-Douglas is also concerned with keeping its F/A-18A Hornet program current through Advanced Hornet upgrades. One of the bigger improvements planned for the Hornet is the addition of the Hughes Aircraft FLIR (Forward-Looking Infrared) navigational system. Falling under the Advanced Hornet program will also be an improved AMRAAM system (along with an AGM-65K Maverick ASM launch system) and more powerful engines. Coupled with the more efficient engines will be increased fuel capacity and a Halon gas fire and damage suppression system.

Mission Setup.
Select Game Mode.
Press 2.
Choose Skill Level.
Press 9.
Select Aircraft Type.
Press 1.
Select Armament.
Press 3 zero times. Total 4.
Press 4 three times. Total 0.
Press 5.

Your Advanced Hornet has a top speed of Mach 1.8 at a maximum altitude of 60,000 feet.

The afterburner, Radar System Display, and Weapon Tracking Indicator may be used during this scenario.

Your armament is one 20mm M61A1 cannon with 500 rounds of ammunition mounted in the jet's nose and four AGM-65K Maverick ASMs carried on external stores.

Mission Objectives. Test the Advanced Hornet's ground strike capabilities.

Flying the Mission.
Step 1 Take off from the aircraft carrier.
Step 2. Never exceed an indicated airspeed of Mach 1.8 or an altitude of 60,000 feet.
Step 3. Climb to an altitude of 1,000 feet.
Step 4. Locate the practice target on your radar.
Step 5. Attack and sink the vessel. Evade all enemy SAM fire.
Step 6. Return to the carrier and land.

Mission Debriefing. You will have successfully flown this mission if you:

☐ Stayed within the performance boundaries of the Advanced Hornet.
☐ Completed the AGM-65K Maverick test.
☐ Safely completed the mission. If you take a hit, be sure to use your Halon gas fire and damage suppression system. McDonnell Douglas would appreciate an actual combat field report on this system's effectiveness.

71. STRIKE

Your F-16A airfield in England has just received a scramble alert. Fifty Warsaw Pact armored divisions are sprinting across northern Italy. Also, a diversionary assault from 32 Soviet divisions is flooding through Helmstedt into the Central Sector of eastern Europe. Only by using constant ground strikes can the advance be held in check until the NATO forces can regroup for a counteroffensive.

Mission Setup.
Select Game Mode.
Press 2.
Choose Skill Level.
Press 1.
Select Aircraft Type.
Press 2.
Select Armament.
Press 3 zero times. Total 4.
Press 4 five times. Total 2.
Press 5.

Your F-16A has a top speed of Mach 2 at a maximum altitude of 60,000 feet.

The afterburner, Radar System Display, and Weapon Tracking Indicator may be used during this scenario.

Your armament is one 20mm M61A1 cannon with 500 rounds of ammunition mounted in the jet's nose and two MK-84 2,000lb bombs and four AGM-65E Maverick ASMs carried on external stores.

Mission Objectives. Fly as many sorties as you can until you lose three aircraft.
Flying the Mission.
Step 1. Take off from runway 22L.
Step 2. Never exceed an indicated airspeed of Mach 2 or an altitude of 60,000 feet.
Step 3. Locate the target on your radar.
Step 4. Destroy the target and return to base to rearm.
Step 5. Repeat the above steps until your third and final F-16A has been shot down.
Mission Debriefing. Score your results:

☐ 0—3 Targets destroyed: NATO can forget it; you'd better learn to speak Russian.
☐ 4—9 Targets destroyed: NATO mustered one French farmer with a pitchfork.
☐ 10—20 Targets destroyed: Resistance to the advance is mounting.
☐ 21—30 Targets destroyed: The Soviet advance has been halted.
☐ 31—50 Targets destroyed: NATO forces are on the offensive; victory will be ours.

72. PERSIAN GULF SHOWDOWN

Your carrier task force has been spotted by the land-based Soviet FA (*Frontovaya Aviatsiya*) air force enemy in the Persian Gulf. Flying from Southern TVD airfields located in Iraq, Syria, and Iran, Soviet MiGs are taking off in round-the-clock flights. Present reports indicate a force of nearly 100 aircraft is approaching the task force. For the moment, the enemy aircraft are fighters, intent on crushing the task force's air defense CAP. Only through repeated launches and dogfights can the destruction of the task force be averted.

Mission Setup.
Select Game Mode.
Press 1.
Choose Skill Level.

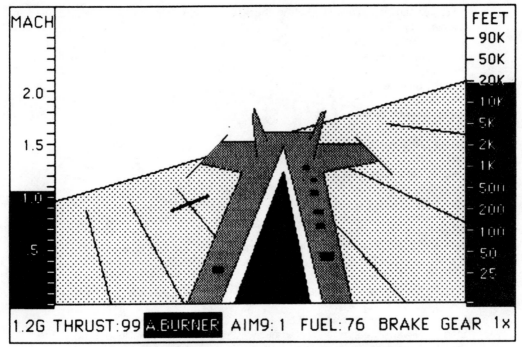

MACH | FEET
2.0
1.5
1.0
.5

90K
50K
20K
10K
5K
2K
1K
500
200
100
50
25

1.2G THRUST:99 A.BURNER AIM9:1 FUEL:76 BRAKE GEAR 1×

Fig. 11-2. With 16 kills, this F/A-18 pilot has a good chance of defending the fleet.

Press 1.
Select Aircraft Type.
Press 1.
Select Armament.
Press 1 five times. Total 2.
Press 2 zero times. Total 4.
Press 5.
Your F/A-18A has a top speed of Mach 1.8 at a maximum altitude of 60,000 feet.

The afterburner, Radar System Display, and Weapon Tracking Indicator may be used during this scenario.

Your armament is one 20mm M61A1 cannon with 500 rounds of ammunition mounted in the jet's nose and two AIM-9L Sidewinder and four AIM-7F Sparrow AAMs carried on external stores.

Mission Objectives. Shoot down as many enemy jets as possible before you crash your F/A-18A three times (Fig. 11-2).

Flying the Mission.
Step 1. Take off from the aircraft carrier.
Step 2. Never exceed an indicated airspeed of Mach 1.8 or an altitude of 60,000 feet.
Step 3. Locate the enemy aircraft on your radar.
Step 4. Shoot down the jets and return to the carrier to rearm.
Step 5. Repeat the above steps until you have crashed your Hornet three times.
Mission Debriefing. Your final score is:

☐ 0—5 Aircraft destroyed: Abandon ship.

☐ 6—15 Aircraft destroyed: The task force is still in deep water.
☐ 16—30 Aircraft destroyed: You'd better return to Miramar for further training.
☐ 31—50 Aircraft destroyed: The sailors can remove their life vests.
☐ 51—80 Aircraft destroyed: Any threat of losing the task force has been removed.
☐ 81+ Aircraft destroyed: Ace of aces; stand by for a port call.

Chapter 12

Breaking Records

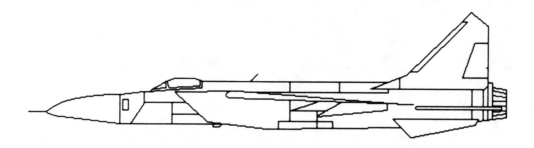

73. SPEED RECORD 1947

Colonel Albert Boyd flying an experimental Lockheed XP-80R Shooting Star set a speed record of 623.855 mph on 19 June 1947.

Mission Setup.
Select Game Mode.
Press 3.
Choose Skill Level.
Press 9.
Select Aircraft Type.
Press 2.

The afterburner, Radar System Display, and Weapon Tracking Indicator may not be used during this scenario.

Optional subLOGIC Scenery Disks can be used for background during this scenario. The lack of an accurate Fuel Quantity Indicator limits the realism with the Scenery Disks, however.

Mission Objectives. Break the 1947 speed record.

Flying the Mission.

Step 1. Take off from runway 0.

Step 2. Stay below an altitude of 400 feet.

Step 3. Do not use the afterburner. Fly in a level attitude and hold your speed for one minute. You must fly faster than Mach .71.

Step 4. Land on runway 0.

Step 5. Taxi into the hangar.

Mission Debriefing. You will have successfully flown this mission if you:

☐ Broke the 1947 speed record.
☐ Safely completed the mission.

74. SPEED RECORD 1952

Lt. Colonel William F. Barnes established a new speed record by flying a North American F-86D Sabre jet at 715.693 mph.
Mission Setup.
Select Game Mode.
Press 3.
Choose Skill Level.
Press 2.
Select Aircraft Type.
Press 2.
The afterburner, Radar System Display, and Weapon Tracking Indicator may not be used during this scenario.
Optional subLOGIC Scenery Disks can be used for background during this scenario. The lack of an accurate Fuel Quantity Indicator limits the realism with the Scenery Disks, however.
Mission Objectives. Break the 1952 speed record.
Flying the Mission.
Step 1. Take off from runway 0.
Step 2. Stay below an altitude of 1,000 feet.
Step 3. Do not use the afterburner. Fly in a level attitude and hold your speed for one minute. You must fly faster than Mach .82.
Step 4. Land on runway 0.
Step 5. Taxi into the hangar.
Mission Debriefing. You will have successfully flown this mission if you:

☐ Broke the 1952 speed record.
☐ Safely completed the mission.

75. SPEED RECORD 1953

Lt. Colonel F. K. Everest set a new speed record on 29 October 1953 by taking a North American YF-100A Super Sabre jet to 755.150 mph.
Mission Setup.
Select Game Mode.
Press 3.
Choose Skill Level.
Press 7.
Select Aircraft Type.
Press 2.
The afterburner and Weapon Tracking Indicator may be used during this scenario.
Optional subLOGIC Scenery Disks can be used for background during this scenario. The lack of an accurate Fuel Quantity Indicator limits the realism with the Scenery Disks, however.
Mission Objectives. Break the 1953 speed record.

Flying the Mission.

Step 1. Take off from runway 0.

Step 2. Stay below an altitude of 500 feet.

Step 3. Do not use the afterburner. Fly in a level attitude and hold your speed for 1 minute. You must fly faster than Mach .99.

Step 4. Land on runway 0.

Step 5. Taxi into the hangar.

Mission Debriefing. You will have successfully flown this mission if you:

☐ Broke the 1953 speed record.

☐ Safely completed the mission.

76. SPEED RECORD 1957

Major Adrian E. Drew flew at 1,207.633 mph on 12 December 1957 in a McDonnell F-101A Voodoo.

Mission Setup.

Select Game Mode.

Press 3.

Choose Skill Level.

Press 4.

Select Aircraft Type.

Press 2.

The afterburner and Weapon Tracking Indicator may be used during this scenario.

Optional subLOGIC Scenery Disks can be used for background during this scenario. The lack of an accurate Fuel Quantity Indicator limits the realism with the Scenery Disks, however.

Mission Objectives. Break the 1957 speed record.

Flying the Mission.

Step 1. Take off from runway 0.

Step 2. Stay below an altitude of 5,000 feet.

Step 3. You may use the afterburner. Fly in a level attitude and hold your speed for one minute. You must fly faster than Mach 1.59.

Step 4. Land on runway 0.

Step 5. Taxi into the hangar.

Mission Debriefing. You will have successfully flown this mission if you:

☐ Broke the 1957 speed record.

☐ Safely completed the mission.

77. ALTITUDE RECORD 1958

Lt. Commander George C. Watkins climbed a Grumman F11F-1F Tiger to an altitude record of 76,932 feet on 18 April 1958.

150

Mission Setup.
Select Game Mode.
Press 3.
Choose Skill Level.
Press 4.
Select Aircraft Type.
Press 1.
The afterburner and Weapon Tracking Indicator may be used during this scenario.
Optional subLOGIC Scenery Disks can be used for background during this scenario. The lack of an accurate Fuel Quantity Indicator limits the realism with the Scenery Disks, however.

Mission Objectives. Break the 1958 altitude record.

Flying the Mission.

Step 1. Take off from the aircraft carrier.
Step 2. Climb to an altitude higher than the 1958 record.
Step 3. You may use the afterburner. Fly in a level attitude at the new altitude and hold your speed for one minute.
Step 4. Land on the carrier.

Mission Debriefing. You will have successfully flown this mission if you:

☐ Broke the 1958 altitude record.
☐ Safely completed the mission.

78. TIME-TO-HEIGHT RECORD 1974

Svetlana Savitskaia flew a Mikoyan-Gurevich E-66B (MiG-25) to a new time-to-height record in 1974 with the following times: 9,900 feet in 41.2 sec.; 19,800 feet in 1 min. .1 sec.; 29,700 feet in 1 min. 21 sec.; 39,600 feet in 1 min. 59.3 sec.

Mission Setup.
Select Game Mode.
Press 3.
Choose Skill Level.
Press 7.
Select Aircraft Type.
Press 2.
Only the Weapon Tracking Indicator may be used during this scenario.
The afterburner may not be used.
Optional subLOGIC Scenery Disks can be used for background during this scenario. The lack of an accurate Fuel Quantity Indicator limits the realism with the Scenery Disks, however.

Mission Objectives. Break the time-to-height record for 1974.

Flying the Mission.
Step 1. Take off from runway 0.
Step 2. Perform your maximum climb.
Step 3. Do not use the afterburner. Clock your times when crossing the following altitudes: 9,900 feet, 19,800 feet, 29,700 feet, and 39,600 feet.
Step 4. Land on runway 0.

Step 5. Taxi into the hangar.

Mission Debriefing. You will have successfully flown this mission if you:

☐ Broke the 1974 time-to-height record.
☐ Safely completed the mission.

79. LOW-ALTITUDE SPEED RECORD 1961

Lts. H. Hardisty and E. De Esch set the low-altitude speed record by flying their McDonnell F4H-1F Phantom II at 902.712 mph on 28 August 1961.

Mission Setup.
Select Game Mode.
Press 3.
Choose Skill Level.
Press 3.
Select Aircraft Type.
Press 2.
The afterburner and Weapon Tracking Indicator may be used during this scenario.
Optional subLOGIC Scenery Disks can be used for background during this scenario. The lack of an accurate Fuel Quantity Indicator limits the realism with the Scenery Disks, however.
Mission Objectives. Break the 1961 speed record.
Flying the Mission.
Step 1. Take off from runway 0.
Step 2. Stay below an altitude of 500 feet.
Step 3. You may use the afterburner. Fly in a level attitude and hold your speed for one minute. You must fly faster than Mach 1.2.
Step 4. Land on runway 0.
Step 5. Taxi into the hangar.
Mission Debriefing. You will have successfully flown this mission if you:

☐ Broke the 1961 speed record.
☐ Safely completed the mission.

80. ALTITUDE WITH PAYLOAD RECORD 1962

Major F. Fulton climbed to an altitude of 85,360.67 feet with 4,400 pounds of payload in a Convair B-58 Hustler on 18 September 1962.

Mission Setup.
Select Game Mode.
Press 2. (This is merely for adding a payload to the aircraft.)
Choose Skill Level.
Press 0.

152

Select Aircraft Type.

Press 1.

Select Armament.

Press 3 two times. Total 6.

Press 4 zero times. Total 4.

Press 5.

Total payload: 4760 pounds

The afterburner and Weapon Tracking Indicator may be used during this scenario.

Optional subLOGIC Scenery Disks can be used for background during this scenario. The lack of an accurate Fuel Quantity Indicator limits the realism with the Scenery Disks, however.

Mission Objectives. Break the 1962 altitude with payload record.

Flying Mission.

Step 1. Take off from the aircraft carrier.

Step 2. Climb to an altitude higher than the 1962 record.

Step 3. You may use the afterburner. Fly in a level attitude at the new altitude and hold your speed for one minute.

Step 4. Land on the carrier.

Mission Debriefing. You will have successfully flown this mission if you:

☐ Broke the 1962 altitude with payload record.

☐ Safely completed the mission.

81. ALTITUDE WITH PAYLOAD RECORD 1973

Colonel Alexander M. Fedotov carried 4,400 pounds to an altitude of 115,584 feet on 25 July 1973 in a Mikoyan-Gurevich E-266 (MiG-25).

Mission Setup.

Select Game Mode.

Press 2. (This is merely for adding a payload to the aircraft.)

Choose Skill Level.

Press 0.

Select Aircraft Type.

Press 2.

Select Armament.

Press 3 two times. Total 6.

Press 4 zero times. Total 4.

Press 5.

Total payload: 4760 pounds.

The afterburner and Weapon Tracking Indicator may be used during this scenario.

Optional subLOGIC Scenery Disks can be used for background during this scenario. The lack of an accurate Fuel Quantity Indicator limits the realism with the Scenery Disks, however.

Mission Objectives. Break the 1973 altitude with payload record.

Flying the Mission.

Step 1. Take off from runway 0.

Step 2. Climb to an altitude higher than the 1973 record.

Step 3. You may use the afterburner. Fly in a level attitude at the new altitude and hold your speed for one minute.

Step 4. Land on runway 0.

Step 5. Taxi into the hangar for some vodka.

Mission Debriefing. You will have successfully flown this mission if you:

☐ Broke the 1973 altitude with payload record.

☐ Safely completed the mission.

82. STRAIGHT LINE SPEED RECORD 1976

Captain Eldon W. Joersz and Major George T. Morgan, Jr., captured the straight line speed record on 28 July 1976 in a Lockheed SR-71A Blackbird flying at 2,193.17 mph.

Mission Setup.

Select Game Mode.

Press 3.

Choose Skill Level.

Press 3.

Select Aircraft Type.

Press 2.

The afterburner and Weapon Tracking Indicator may be used during this scenario.

Optional subLOGIC Scenery Disks can be used for background during this scenario. The

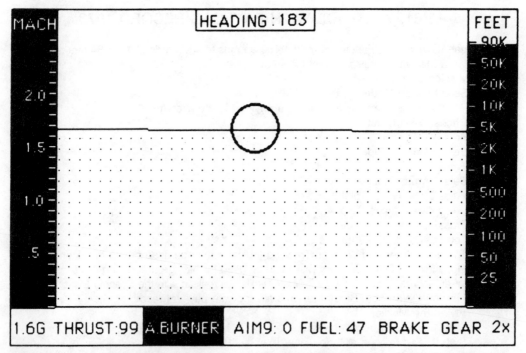

Fig. 12-1. Meeting the speed requirements for breaking the 1976 straight line speed record can only be estimated with the JET Airspeed Indicator. Use this HUD example as a guide for meeting this mission's objectives.

lack of an accurate Fuel Quantity Indicator limits the realism with the Scenery Disks, however.

Mission Objectives. Break the 1976 straight line speed record.

Flying the Mission.

Step 1. Take off from runway 0.

Step 2. Stay below an altitude of 90,000 feet.

Step 3. You may use the afterburner. Fly in a level attitude and hold your speed for one minute. You must fly faster than Mach 2.89 (Fig. 12-1).

Step 4. Land on runway 0.

Step 5. Taxi into the hangar.

Mission Debriefing. You will have successfully flown this mission if you:

☐ Broke the 1976 straight line speed record.
☐ Safely completed the mission.

Appendix A

Annotated Reviews of Flight Simulation Software

The sheer number of flight simulation programs in today's marketplace is indicative of the popularity of this type of software. Very few other genres of software can boast such a large following. This includes entertainment type packages, as well as those used in more profitable business pursuits.

In order to help you better evaluate this enormous aerial offering, all of the major flight simulation software packages have been assembled into this appendix. By definition, ''major flight simulation software'' refers to those products that can be readily purchased at either a local level or through mail-order companies. Granted, many public domain and independent manufacturers' programs exist, but their long-term availability is unpredictable.

AcroJet

Microprose Software
120 Lakefront Drive
Hunt Valley, MD 21030
(301) 667-1151

Version Tested: Commodore 64 w/64K RAM.
Comments: What is billed as an ''advanced flight simulator'' turns out to be nothing more than an accelerated version of Solo Flight (see below). With AcroJet, however, you are flying a Bede BD-5J single-seat, lightweight, turbojet-powered aircraft. By using a detached silhouette view of the BD-5J, you fly through 10 boring aerial aerobatic maneuvers.

AIRSIM-3

Mind Systems Corp.
P.O. Box 506
Northampton, MA 01061
(413) 586-6463

Version Tested: Apple IIe w/128K RAM.

Comments: With 50 different commands to master, AIRSIM-3 is one of the more powerful flight simulation programs currently available. Poor documentation and the lack of a fuel gauge limit the amount of pleasure that can be derived from this program.

Captain Goodnight and the Islands of Fear

Broderbund Software, Inc.
17 Paul Drive
San Rafael, CA 94903
(415) 479-1170

Version Tested: Apple IIe w/128K RAM.

Comments: Captain Goodnight is an extreme departure from all of the other flight simulation software that is mentioned in this appendix. Based loosely on the serial action movies from the 1930s and 1940s, only several "real" flight simulation scenes appear during Captain Goodnight's adventure. The good captain's piloting skills are tested in a high-performance jet fighter, a slow-moving piston-powered transport, and an armed helicopter. In each case, poor flying techniques will result in a crash. If nothing else, Captain Goodnight is an enjoyable diversion from the tense drama of JET combat.

Eagles

Strategic Simulations, Inc.
883 Stierlin Road
Building A-200
Mountain View, CA 94043
(415) 964-1200

Versions Tested: Apple IIe w/128K RAM and Atari 800XL w/40K RAM.

Comments: While not a flight simulation program in the same mold as the others presented in this appendix, Eagles does provide many enjoyable hours of historic World War I action. There are several other programs that follow this same flight simulation approach. Another program that follows in Eagles' footsteps, Europe Ablaze, is equally entertaining, except it is in the World War II scheme of things.

F-15 Strike Eagle

Microprose Software
120 Lakefront Drive
Hunt Valley, MD 21030
(301) 667-1151

Versions Tested: Apple IIe w/128K RAM and IBM PC XT w/640K RAM.

Comments: This is a baffling program. It continually rides the loftier reaches of the computer software bestsellers' list, yet it offers some of the poorest execution found in today's flight simulation software. For example, many of the performance specifications of the F-15 can be stressed beyond their reasonable limits and this bird will keep flying. Even landing the F-15 after a mission is an equally ludicrous affair. All you have to do is pass over a triangle at any speed under an altitude of 3000 feet. Forget about lowering your landing gear; there isn't any.

Flight Simulator/Flight Simulator II

subLOGIC Corporation
713 Edgebrook Drive
Champaign, IL 61830
(217) 359-8482

Versions Tested: Amiga w/256K RAM, Apple IIe w/128K RAM, Atari 800XL w/40K RAM, Commodore 64 w/64K RAM, IBM PC XT w/640K RAM, Macintosh w/512K RAM.

Comments: This is the program that started the rush for flight simulation software. None of the other programs discussed in this appendix approaches either the complexity or the realism that is present in Flight Simulator and Flight Simulator II. A companion volume to this book, *Flight Simulator and Flight Simulator II: 82 Challenging New Adventures* TAB book No. 2862, provides detailed instruction for flying this program.

Fokker Triplane Flight Simulator

PBI Software
1155B-H Chess Drive
Foster City, CA 94404
(415) 349-8765

Version Tested: Macintosh w/512K RAM.

Comments: Flying a World War I vintage Fokker DR.I Triplane has never looked so good. All of the performance that was found in the original has been adequately duplicated in this computer-based version. Aerobatics, balloon-busting, and dogfights are all elements of Fokker Triplane Flight Simulator. The ability to land at various sites and alter weather conditions raises this dogfighter above many of its contemporaries.

Harrier Strike Mission

Miles Computing, Inc.
21018 Osborne Street
Building 5
Canoga Park, CA 91304
(818) 341-1411

Version Tested: Macintosh w/512K RAM.

Comments: A limitation in the number of different missions available to the AV-8A Harrier pilot makes Harrier Strike Mission a very narrow flight simulator. There are two different skill levels with an optional day or night mission performance condition. The execution and realism of Harrier Strike Mission are topnotch, but the lack of mission depth hampers the survivability of this simulator.

JET

subLOGIC Corporation
713 Edgebrook Drive
Champaign, IL 61830
(217) 359-8482

Versions Tested: Apple IIe w/128K RAM, Commodore 64 w/64K RAM, IBM PC XT w/640K RAM.

Comments: SubLOGIC brings all of the sophistication of Flight Simulator II into the modern jet age. Piloting high-performance versions of the U.S. Air Force's F-16 and U.S. Navy's F/A-18 in numerous tactical and strategic situations form the premise of JET.

MacChallenger

Aegis Development, Inc.
Suite 277
2210 Wilshire Blvd.
Santa Monica, CA 90403
(213) 306-0735

Version Tested: Macintosh w/512K RAM.

Comments: MacChallenger proves that beautiful graphics can't support a weak concept. Instead of taking a space shuttle through its entire launch, orbit, and recovery phases, Mac-Challenger just shoots landings at either Edwards AFB or the Cape. There is one nice feature in this program, however. A special ''recording camera'' films each of the shuttle landings. Later, this footage can be reviewed from one of 10 different camera perspectives.

Rendezvous

EDUWare Services, Inc.
185 Berry Street
San Francisco, CA 94107
(415) 546-1937

Version Tested: Apple IIe w/128K RAM.

Comments: This is an educational program based on a fictitious space shuttle mission. The low-quality graphics and heavy emphasis on mathematical skills makes this program unattractive for home pilot use.

Skyfox

Electronic Arts
2755 Campus Drive
San Mateo, CA 94403
(415) 571-7171

Version Tested: Apple IIe w/128K RAM.

Comments: If you can overlook the fantasy aspects of this program, then you are in for a real ride. Excellent graphics, superb sound, and precision flight characteristics are all prime features of Skyfox. There's even a special arcade game, Alpha Invaders, hidden inside Skyfox. Just trying to discover this secret bonus will be enjoyment enough for some people.

Solo Flight

Microprose Software
120 Lakefront Drive
Hunt Valley, MD 21030
(301) 667-1151

Versions Tested: Apple //e w/128K RAM and IBM PC XT w/640K RAM.
Comments: Solo Flight offers two different methods of simulation. One is a small civilian-type craft that has four different modes of flight: clear weather, landing practice, windy conditions, and IFR. The second simulation is Mail Pilot. Mail Pilot is a game where the computer user must fly the aircraft to various locations carrying differing amounts of mail. Unfortunately, none of your flying, with either method, is from a cockpit perspective. Actually, you're flying an aircraft silhouette several hundred feet in front of your view.

Space Shuttle—A Journey Into Space

Activision
P.O. Box 7287
Mountain View, CA 94039
(800) 227-9759

Version Tested: Apple //e w/128K RAM.
Comments: This is by far the finest space simulation that you will ever fly. All of the sights, sounds, and thrills of flying a space shuttle can be found in this game. Space Shuttle is supported by some of the best documentation found in flight simulation programming.

Spitfire Simulator

Mind Systems Corp.
P.O. Box 506
Northampton, MA 01061
(413) 586-6463

Version Tested: Apple //e w/128K RAM.
Comments: If you can overlook the minimal documentation, vector graphics, and the odd positioning for the joystick, then Spitfire Simulator will take you into the wild blue yonder of the skies over England during the Battle of Britain. Takeoffs, landings, fuel consumption, and Messerschmitts—it's all available in Spitfire Simulator.

Stunt Flyer

Sierra Online
P.O. Box 485
Coatsegold, CA 93614

Version Tested: Commodore 64 w/64K RAM.

Comments: Several nice features make this modest flight simulator worth a careful look. There are three choices for flight: air show, free flight, and stunt flying. The stunt flying option presents the greatest attraction with Stunt Flyer. After selecting your stunt from a menu, you take to the air and execute your selection. Following your attempt, a special replay feature shows your performance from a ground observer's vantage point. Unfortunately, the poor graphics and awful sound negate many of the pulses found in Stunt Flyer.

Super Huey

Cosmi, Inc.
415 N. Figueroa Street
Wilmington, CA 90744

Version Tested: Commodore 64 w/64K RAM.

Comments: Four different graphic scenarios taken from the cockpit of a Super Huey helicopter. Both the rescue and combat missions generate the greatest degree of excitement. Both the graphics and sound capabilities of the Commodore 64 are realistically exploited in Super Huey.

Tranquility Base

EDUWare Services, Inc.
185 Berry Street
San Francisco, CA 94107
(415) 546-1937

Version Tested: Apple //e w/128K RAM.

Comments: Tranquility Base tests your skill at flying a NASA Lunar Excursion Module (LEM) around America's first lunar colony. This program's intended education scope stresses the physics of gravitation and motion. Therefore, users after a more thrilling bit of flight simulation should consider piloting one of the other programs listed in this appendix instead of becoming lost in space at Tranquility Base.

Miscellaneous

Ace of Aces by Accolade Software.
B-1 Nuclear Bomber by Avalon Hill Software.
Beach Head by Access Software.
Beachhead II by Access Software.
The Dam Busters by Accolade.
50 Mission Crush by Strategic Simulations, Inc.
Hellcat Ace by Microprose Software.
Jet Combat Simulator by Epyx Software.
Jump Jet by Avant-Garde Creations.
Raid Over Moscow by Access Software.
Spitfire Ace by Microprose Software.
Spitfire '40 by Avalon Hill Software.
Zaxxon by Datasoft, Inc.

Comments: There are numerous games that function in the environment of a flight simulation situation. These games offer a great degree of excitement, usually, at the expense of realism.

Appendix B

Writing Your Own Flight Simulation Program

This appendix contains complete computer program listings, for several popular personal microcomputer types, describing a simple flight simulator. Each of these programs is written in the elementary computer language, BASIC (Beginner's All-purpose Symbolic Instruction Code). No special provisions will be necessary for running these programs. Only the keyboard and the standard amount of memory inherent to each particular computer type is required.

Begin by typing in the program *exactly* as it appears in the listing that matches your brand of computer. Any deviations from the listing could result in a "crashed" computer. Make sure that the computer's Caps Lock key is engaged during this program entry stage. Since an introduction into computer programming is beyond the scope of this appendix, all explanatory remark statements have been removed from each program listing. Believe me, if you type the program into your computer exactly as it is printed in these listings, it will work properly. Trust me.

Once you have entered the complete program listing, double-check your typing. Catching an error at this time will prevent disappointments later. Now save the program on a suitable medium. This step must be performed before your first "test flight." Assign the name FLY ME to your saved BASIC program file.

Seven basic flight control actions are simulated in this program: level flight, climb, dive, bank-left, bank-right, landing gear operation, and weapons launching. The keyboard keys for performing these actions are:

    N = normal flight
    M = climb
    I = dive
    J = bank-left
    K = bank-right
    G = landing gear Up/Down
    F = weapons launch
    S = stop

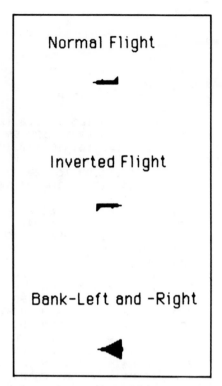

Fig. B-1. Three of the flight silhouettes used in the FLY ME BASIC program.

Normal Flight

Inverted Flight

Bank-Left and -Right

Each of these keyboard commands requires an upper case key entry. Therefore, the computer's Caps Lock key must be depressed during operation of FLY ME. In order to retain the highest degree of realism, always begin and end all of your flight maneuvers from the normal flight attitude. Figure B-1 shows FLY ME in several flight attitudes. Failure to follow this simple rule will result in some rather ridiculous flight patterns. For example;

The Right Way:
A loop—press M three times; M + M + M.
The Wrong Way:
A loop—press M followed by N three times; M + N + M + N + M + N.

The major benefit of FLY ME is its rendering of a detached visual accounting of the basic aircraft controls used in JET. By working with this short program, you will develop a better understanding of the forces that are being exerted on your aircraft as you exercise a specific aerial maneuver. Of course, after you have mastered FLY ME, you can add some of your own programming for simulating actual takeoffs and landings.

Listing B-1. FLY ME for the Apple II family of computers.

```
5    HOME
10   G = 0:I = 0:M = 0:J = 0:K$ = " "
20   HGR
30   POKE  - 16302,0
40   HCOLOR= 3
50   HPLOT 100,100 TO 120,100
60   HPLOT 103,99 TO 120,99
70   HPLOT 103,101 TO 120,101
80   HPLOT 108,98
90   HPLOT 118,97 TO 120,97
100  HPLOT 117,98 TO 120,98
110  HPLOT 120,96
120 P =  PEEK ( - 16336)
130 K =  PEEK ( - 16384)
140  IF K > 127 THEN  GOTO 200
150  GOTO 120
200  GET K$
210  IF K$ = "N" THEN  GOTO 20
220  IF K$ = "S" THEN  TEXT : END
230  IF K$ = "M" THEN  GOTO 300
240  IF K$ = "I" THEN  GOTO 400
250  IF K$ = "J" THEN  GOTO 500
260  IF K$ = "K" THEN  GOTO 500
270  IF K$ = "G" THEN  GOTO 600
280  IF K$ = "F" THEN  GOTO 700
290  IF K$ <  > "N" OR K$ <  > "S" OR K$ <  > "I" OR K$ <  > "M" OR K$ <
       > "J" OR K$ <  > "K" OR K$ <  > "G" OR K$ <  > "F" THEN  GOTO 120
300 I = I + 1
302  HGR
304  IF I = 2 THEN  GOTO 330
306  IF I = 3 THEN  GOTO 350
308  IF I = 4 THEN I = 0: GOTO 20
310  HPLOT 105,85 TO 120,100
312  HPLOT 108,87 TO 120,99
314  HPLOT 107,88 TO 119,100
316  HPLOT 113,90
318  HPLOT 118,96 TO 121,99
320  HPLOT 120,97 TO 122,99
322  HPLOT 122,98
324  GOTO 120
330  HGR
332  HPLOT 120,80 TO 120,100
334  HPLOT 119,83 TO 119,100
336  HPLOT 121,83 TO 121,100
338  HPLOT 122,88
340  HPLOT 122,97 TO 122,100
342  HPLOT 123,98 TO 123,100
344  HPLOT 124,100
346  GOTO 120
350  HGR
352  HPLOT 120,100 TO 140,100
354  HPLOT 120,99 TO 137,99
356  HPLOT 120,101 TO 137,101
358  HPLOT 132,102
360  HPLOT 120,102 TO 123,102
```

```
362    HPLOT 120,103 TO 122,103
364    HPLOT 120,104
366    GOTO 120
400  M = M + 1
402    HGR
404    IF M = 2 THEN  GOTO 430
406    IF M = 3 THEN  GOTO 350
408    IF M = 4 THEN M = 0: GOTO 20
410    HPLOT 105,115 TO 120,100
412    HPLOT 108,113 TO 120,101
414    HPLOT 107,112 TO 119,100
416    HPLOT 110,108
418    HPLOT 116,102 TO 119,99
420    HPLOT 117,100 TO 119,98
422    HPLOT 118,98
424    GOTO 120
430    HGR
432    HPLOT 120,100 TO 120,120
434    HPLOT 119,100 TO 119,117
436    HPLOT 121,100 TO 121,117
438    HPLOT 118,112
440    HPLOT 118,100 TO 118,103
442    HPLOT 117,100 TO 117,102
444    HPLOT 116,100
446    GOTO 120
500    HGR
501  J = J + 1
502    IF J = 2 THEN  GOTO 530
504    IF J = 3 THEN  GOTO 550
506    IF J = 4 THEN  GOTO 570
508    IF J = 5 THEN  GOTO 530
509    IF J = 6 THEN J = 0: GOTO 20
510    HPLOT 100,100 TO 120,100
511    HPLOT 103,99 TO 120,99
512    HPLOT 103,101 TO 120,101
513    HPLOT 108,98 TO 119,98
514    HPLOT 110,97 TO 119,97
515    HPLOT 112,96 TO 119,96
516    HPLOT 114,95 TO 119,95
517    HPLOT 116,94 TO 119,94
518    HPLOT 118,93 TO 119,93
519    HPLOT 108,102 TO 119,102
520    HPLOT 110,103 TO 119,103
521    HPLOT 112,104 TO 119,104
522    HPLOT 114,105 TO 119,105
523    HPLOT 116,106 TO 119,106
524    HPLOT 118,107 TO 119,107
525    GOTO 120
530    HGR
531    HPLOT 115,100 TO 130,100
532    HPLOT 119,97 TO 119,100
533    HPLOT 126,97 TO 126,100
534    HPLOT 122,99 TO 123,99
535    GOTO 120
550    HGR
551    HPLOT 120,100 TO 140,100
552    HPLOT 120,99 TO 137,99
553    HPLOT 120,101 TO 137,101
```

```
554    HPLOT 132,98
555    HPLOT 120,98 TO 123,98
556    HPLOT 120,97 TO 122,97
557    HPLOT 120,96
558    GOTO 120
570    HGR
571    HPLOT 120,100 TO 140,100
572    HPLOT 120,99 TO 137,99
573    HPLOT 120,101 TO 137,101
574    HPLOT 121,98 TO 132,98
575    HPLOT 121,97 TO 130,97
576    HPLOT 121,96 TO 128,96
577    HPLOT 121,95 TO 126,95
578    HPLOT 121,94 TO 124,94
579    HPLOT 121,93 TO 122,93
580    HPLOT 121,102 TO 132,102
581    HPLOT 121,103 TO 130,103
582    HPLOT 121,104 TO 128,104
583    HPLOT 121,105 TO 126,105
584    HPLOT 121,106 TO 124,106
585    HPLOT 121,107 TO 122,107
586    GOTO 120
600    HGR
601 G = G + 1
602    IF G = 2 THEN G = 0: GOTO 20
604    HPLOT 100,100 TO 120,100
606    HPLOT 103,99 TO 120,99
608    HPLOT 103,101 TO 120,101
610    HPLOT 108,98
612    HPLOT 118,97 TO 120,97
614    HPLOT 117,98 TO 120,98
616    HPLOT 120,96
618    HPLOT 104,102 TO 104,103
620    HPLOT 112,102 TO 112,103
622    GOTO 120
700    HGR
702    HPLOT 100,100 TO 120,100
704    HPLOT 103,99 TO 120,99
706    HPLOT 103,101 TO 120,101
708    HPLOT 108,98
710    HPLOT 118,97 TO 120,97
712    HPLOT 117,98 TO 120,98
714    HPLOT 120,96
716    PRINT  CHR$ (7)
720    FOR X = 1 TO 99
722    HPLOT 100 - X,101 TO 103 - X,101
724 P =  PEEK ( - 16336)
726    HCOLOR= 0
728    HPLOT 100 - X,101 TO 103 - X,101
730    HCOLOR= 3
732    NEXT X
734    GOTO 120
```

Listing B-2. FLY ME for the IBM PC family of computers.

```
10 KEY OFF
20 G=0:I=0:M=0:J=0:K$=""
30 CLS:SCREEN 1:COLOR ,1
40 LINE (100,100)-(120,100)
50 LINE (103,99)-(120,99)
60 LINE (103,101)-(120,101)
70 PSET (108,98)
80 LINE (118,97)-(120,97)
90 LINE (117,98)-(120,98)
100 PSET (120,96)
110 SOUND 40,.1
120 K$=INKEY$
130 IF K$="" THEN 110
200 IF K$="N" THEN 30
210 IF K$="S" THEN KEY ON:SCREEN 0:WIDTH 80:END
220 IF K$="M" THEN 300
230 IF K$="I" THEN 400
240 IF K$="J" THEN 500
250 IF K$="K" THEN 500
260 IF K$="G" THEN 600
270 IF K$="F" THEN 700
280 IF K$<>"N" OR K$<>"S" OR K$<>"I" OR K$<>"M" OR K$<>"J" OR K$<>"K"
        OR K$<>"G" OR K$<>"F" THEN 110
300 I=I+1
302 CLS
304 IF I=2 THEN 330
306 IF I=3 THEN 350
308 IF I=4 THEN I=0:GOTO 30
310 LINE (105,85)-(120,100)
312 LINE (108,87)-(120,99)
314 LINE (107,88)-(119,100)
316 PSET (112,90)
318 LINE (118,96)-(121,99)
320 LINE (120,97)-(122,99)
322 PSET (122,98)
324 GOTO 110
330 CLS
332 LINE (120,80)-(120,100)
334 LINE (119,83)-(119,100)
336 LINE (121,83)-(121,100)
338 PSET (122,88)
340 LINE (122,97)-(122,100)
342 LINE (123,98)-(123,100)
344 PSET (124,100)
346 GOTO 110
350 CLS
352 LINE (120,100)-(140,100)
354 LINE (120,99)-(137,99)
356 LINE (120,101)-(137,101)
358 PSET (132,102)
360 LINE (120,102)-(123,102)
362 LINE (120,103)-(122,103)
364 PSET (120,104)
366 GOTO 110
```

```
400 M=M+1
402 CLS
404 IF M=2 THEN 430
406 IF M=3 THEN 350
408 IF M=4 THEN M=0:GOTO 30
410 LINE (105,115)-(120,100)
412 LINE (108,113)-(120,101)
414 LINE (107,112)-(119,100)
416 PSET (110,108)
418 LINE (116,102)-(119,99)
420 LINE (117,100)-(119,98)
422 PSET (118,98)
424 GOTO 110
430 CLS
432 LINE (120,100)-(120,120)
434 LINE (119,100)-(119,117)
436 LINE (121,100)-(121,117)
438 PSET (118,112)
440 LINE (118,100)-(118,103)
442 LINE (117,100)-(117,102)
444 PSET (116,100)
446 GOTO 110
500 CLS
501 J=J+1
502 IF J=2 THEN 530
504 IF J=3 THEN 550
506 IF J=4 THEN 570
508 IF J=5 THEN 530
509 IF J=6 THEN J=0:GOTO 30
510 LINE (100,100)-(120,100)
511 LINE (103,99)-(120,99)
512 LINE (103,101)-(120,101)
513 LINE (108,98)-(119,98)
514 LINE (110,97)-(119,97)
515 LINE (112,96)-(119,96)
516 LINE (114,95)-(119,95)
517 LINE (116,94)-(119,94)
518 LINE (118,93)-(119,93)
519 LINE (108,102)-(119,102)
520 LINE (110,103)-(119,103)
521 LINE (112,104)-(119,104)
522 LINE (114,105)-(119,105)
523 LINE (116,106)-(119,106)
524 LINE (118,107)-(119,107)
525 GOTO 110
530 CLS
531 LINE (115,100)-(130,100)
532 LINE (119,97)-(119,100)
533 LINE (126,97)-(126,100)
534 LINE (122,99)-(123,99)
535 GOTO 110
550 CLS
551 LINE (120,100)-(140,100)
552 LINE (120,99)-(137,99)
553 LINE (120,101)-(137,101)
554 PSET (132,98)
555 LINE (120,98)-(123,98)
556 LINE (120,97)-(122,97)
```

```
557 PSET (120,96)
558 GOTO 110
570 CLS
571 LINE (120,100)-(140,100)
572 LINE (120,99)-(137,99)
573 LINE (120,101)-(137,101)
574 LINE (121,98)-(132,98)
575 LINE (121,97)-(130,97)
576 LINE (121,96)-(128,96)
577 LINE (121,95)-(126,95)
578 LINE (121,94)-(124,94)
579 LINE (121,93)-(122,93)
580 LINE (121,102)-(132,102)
581 LINE (121,103)-(130,103)
582 LINE (121,104)-(128,104)
583 LINE (121,105)-(126,105)
584 LINE (121,106)-(124,106)
585 LINE (121,107)-(122,107)
586 GOTO 110
600 CLS
601 G=G+1
602 IF G=2 THEN G=0:GOTO 30
604 LINE (100,100)-(120,100)
606 LINE (103,99)-(120,99)
608 LINE (103,101)-(120,101)
610 PSET (108,98)
612 LINE (118,97)-(120,97)
614 LINE (117,98)-(120,98)
616 PSET (120,96)
618 LINE (104,102)-(104,103)
620 LINE (112,102)-(112,103)
622 GOTO 110
700 CLS
702 LINE (100,100)-(120,100)
704 LINE (103,99)-(120,99)
706 LINE (103,101)-(120,101)
708 PSET (108,98)
710 LINE (118,97)-(120,97)
712 LINE (117,98)-(120,98)
714 PSET (120,96)
716 BEEP
720 FOR X=1 TO 99
722 LINE (100-X,101)-(103-X,101),3
724 SOUND 110,.2
726 LINE (100-X,101)-(103-X,101),0
728 NEXT X
730 COLOR ,1
732 GOTO 110
```

Listing B-3. FLY ME for the Macintosh computer.

```
CLS
G=0 :I=0 :M=0 :J=0 :K$=""
NORMAL:
CLS
```

```
    LINE (100,100)-(120,100),33
    LINE (103,99)-(120,99)
    LINE (103,101)-(120,101)
    PSET (108,98)
    LINE (118,97)-(120,97)
    LINE (117,98)-(120,98)
    PSET (120,96)
KEYCHECK:
 SOUND 40,1
 K$=INKEY$
  IF K$="" THEN KEYCHECK
  IF K$="N" THEN NORMAL
  IF K$="S" THEN CLS :END
  IF K$="M" THEN UP
  IF K$="I" THEN DOWN
  IF K$="J" THEN BANK
  IF K$="K" THEN BANK
  IF K$="G" THEN GEAR
  IF K$="F" THEN FIRE
    IF K$<>"N" OR K$<>"S" OR K$<>"I" OR K$<>"M" OR K$<>"J" OR K$<>"K" OR K$<>"G" OR K$<>
    "F" THEN
  KEYCHECK
  UP:
  I=I+1
  CLS
  IF I=2 THEN UPII
  IF I=3 THEN UPIII
  IF I=4 THEN I=0 :GOTO NORMAL
    LINE (105,85)-(120,100)
    LINE (108,87)-(120,99)
    LINE (107,88)-(119,100)
    PSET (112,90)
    LINE (118,96)-(121,99)
    LINE (120,97)-(122,99)
    PSET (122,98)
    GOTO KEYCHECK
  UPII:
  CLS
    LINE (120,80)-(120,100)
    LINE (119,83)-(119,100)
    LINE (121,83)-(121,100)
    PSET (122,88)
    LINE (122,97)-(122,100)
    LINE (123,98)-(123,100)
```

```
   PSET (124,100)
   GOTO KEYCHECK
UPIII:
 CLS
   LINE (120,100)-(140,100)
   LINE (120,99)-(137,99)
   LINE (120,101)-(137,101)
   PSET (132,102)
   LINE (120,102)-(123,102)
   LINE (120,103)-(122,103)
   PSET (120,104)
   GOTO KEYCHECK
DOWN:
 M=M+1
 CLS
  IF M=2 THEN DOWNII
  IF M=3 THEN UPIII
  IF M=4 THEN M=0:GOTO NORMAL
   LINE (105,115)-(120,100)
   LINE (108,113)-(120,101)
   LINE (107,112)-(119,100)
   PSET (110,108)
   LINE (116,102)-(119,99)
   LINE (117,100)-(119,98)
   PSET (118,98)
   GOTO KEYCHECK
DOWNII:
 CLS
   LINE (120,100)-(120,120)
   LINE (119,100)-(119,117)
   LINE (121,100)-(121,117)
   PSET (118,112)
   LINE (118,100)-(118,103)
   LINE (117,100)-(117,102)
   PSET (116,100)
   GOTO KEYCHECK
BANK:
 CLS
 J=J+1
   IF J=2 THEN BANKII
   IF J=3 THEN BANKIII
   IF J=4 THEN BANKIV
   IF J=5 THEN BANKII
```

```
        IF J=6 THEN J=0 :GOTO NORMAL
           LINE (100,100)-(120,100)
           LINE (103,99)-(120,99)
           LINE (103,101)-(120,101)
           LINE (108,98)-(119,98)
           LINE (110,97)-(119,97)
           LINE (112,96)-(119,96)
           LINE (114,95)-(119,95)
           LINE (116,94)-(119,94)
           LINE (118,93)-(119,93)
           LINE (108,102)-(119,102)
           LINE (110,103)-(119,103)
           LINE (112,104)-(119,104)
           LINE (114,105)-(119,105)
           LINE (116,106)-(119,106)
           LINE (118,107)-(119,107)
           GOTO KEYCHECK
   BANKII:
    CLS
         LINE (115,100)-(130,100)
         LINE (119,97)-(119,100)
         LINE (126,97)-(126,100)
         LINE (122,99)-(123,99)
         GOTO KEYCHECK
   BANKIII:
    CLS
         LINE (120,100)-(140,100)
         LINE (120,99)-(137,99)
         LINE (120,101)-(137,101)
         PSET (132,98)
         LINE (120,98)-(123,98)
         LINE (120,97)-(122,97)
         PSET (120,96)
         GOTO KEYCHECK
   BANKIV:
    CLS
         LINE (120,100)-(140,100)
         LINE (120,99)-(137,99)
         LINE (120,101)-(137,101)
         LINE (121,98)-(132,98)
         LINE (121,97)-(130,97)
         LINE (121,96)-(128,96)
         LINE (121,95)-(126,95)
```

```
      LINE (121,94)-(124,94)
      LINE (121,93)-(122,93)
      LINE (121,102)-(132,102)
      LINE (121,103)-(130,103)
      LINE (121,104)-(128,104)
      LINE (121,105)-(126,105)
      LINE (121,106)-(124,106)
      LINE (121,107)-(122,107)
     GOTO KEYCHECK
 GEAR:
  CLS
  G=G+1
   IF G=2 THEN G=0 :GOTO NORMAL
    LINE (100,100)-(120,100)
    LINE (103,99)-(120,99)
    LINE (103,101)-(120,101)
    PSET (108,98)
    LINE (118,97)-(120,97)
    LINE (117,98)-(120,98)
    PSET (120,96)
    LINE (104,102)-(104,103)
    LINE (112,102)-(112,103)
    GOTO KEYCHECK
 FIRE:
  CLS
    LINE (100,100)-(120,100),33
    LINE (103,99)-(120,99)
    LINE (103,101)-(120,101)
    PSET (108,98)
    LINE (118,97)-(120,97)
    LINE (117,98)-(120,98)
    PSET (120,96)
     BEEP
    FOR X=1 TO 99
      LINE (100-X,101)-(103-X,101),33
       SOUND 910,1
      LINE (100-X,101)-(103-X,101),0
    NEXT X
     GOTO KEYCHECK
```

Appendix C

Aircraft Identification Guide

This appendix provides illustrations and performance specifications for many of the aircraft discussed in the Historical Aviation Scenarios found in Part II of this book.

Name: Me 262A-1a.
Manufacturer: Messerschmitt A.G. (Aktiengesellschaft).
Powerplant: Two Junkers Jumo 004B-1, -2, or -3 turbojets, each rated at 1980lb thrust.
Performance: 510 mph at 32,800 feet.
Dimensions: Wingspan, 40 feet 11.5 inches; length, 34 feet 9.5 inches.
Weight: Empty, 8378lb; loaded, 15,720lb.

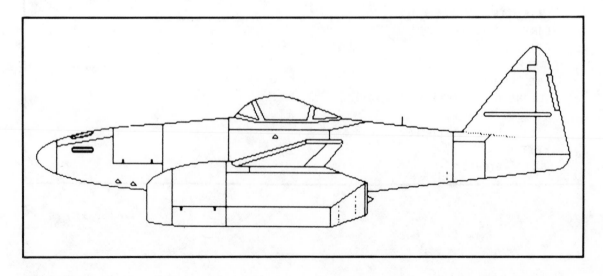

Name: Me 163B-1a.
Manufacturer: Messerschmitt A.G. (Aktiengesellschaft).
Powerplant: One Walter HWK 509A-2 rocket motor rated at 3750lb thrust.
Performance: 596 mph at 30,000 feet.
Dimensions: Wingspan, 30 feet 7.33 inches; length, 19 feet 2.33 inches.
Weight: Empty, 4200lb; loaded, 9500lb.

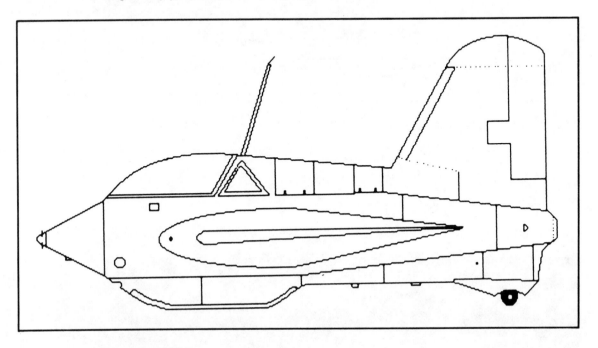

Name: Ar 234B-2
Manufacturer: Arado Flugzeugwerke G.m.b.H. (Gesellschaft mit beschränkter Haftung).
Powerplant: Two Junkers Jumo 004B Orkan turbojets each rated at 1980lb thrust.
Performance: 435 mph at 32,800 feet.
Dimensions: Wingspan, 46 feet 3.5 inches; length, 41 feet 5.5 inches.
Weight: Empty, 11,464lb; loaded, 21,715lb.

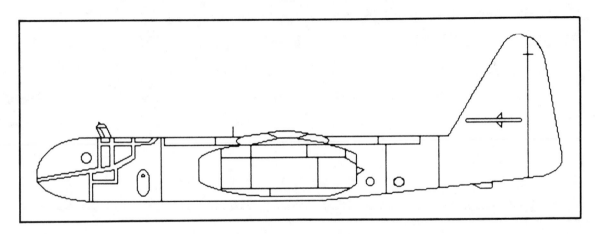

Name: MXY-7
Manufacturer: Yokosuka
Powerplant: Three rocket motors.
Performance: 576 mph in a one-way dive.

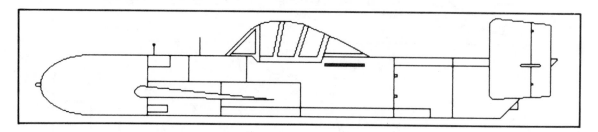

Name: F-80C (A T-33 variant is illustrated.)
Manufacturer: Lockheed.
Powerplant: One GE J33-A-17 turbojet rated at 3750lb thrust.
Performance: 580 mph at 42,750 feet.
Dimensions: Wingspan, 39 feet; length, 34 feet 6 inches.
Weight: Empty, 8240lb; loaded, 15,336lb.

Name: MiG-15.
Manufacturer: Mikoyan-Gurevich.
Powerplant: One Klimov VK-1 turbojet rated at 4000lb thrust.
Performance: 600 mph at 39,370 feet.
Dimensions: Wingspan, 34 feet; length, 35 feet 7.5 inches.
Weight: Empty, 7496lb; loaded, 12,754lb.

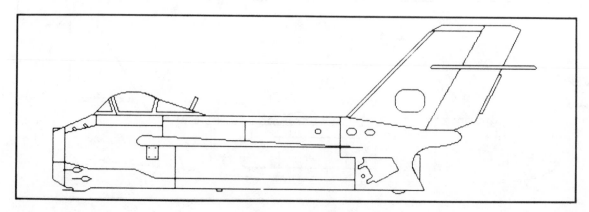

Name: F-86F Sabre.
Manufacturer: North American.
Powerplant: One GE J47-GE-27 turbojet rated at 5970lb thrust.
Performance: 610 mph at 35,000 feet.
Dimensions: Wingspan, 37 feet 1 inch; length, 37 feet 6 inches.
Weight: Empty, 10,950lb; loaded, 17,000lb.

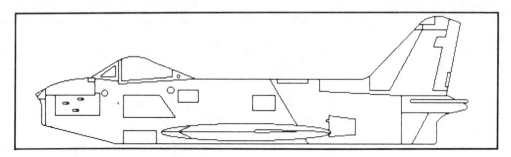

Name: F9F-2 Panther.
Manufacturer: Grumman.
Powerplant: One Pratt & Whitney J42-P-8 turbojet rated at 5750lb thrust.
Performance: 579 mph at 42,800 feet.
Dimensions: Wingspan, 38 feet; length, 37 feet 3 inches.
Weight: Empty, 10,147lb; loaded, 17,766lb.

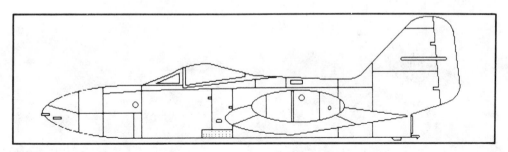

Name: F-84G Thunderjet.
Manufacturer: Republic.
Powerplant: One Allison J35-A-17D turbojet rated at 5600lb thrust.
Performance: 622 mph at 40,500 feet.
Dimensions: Wingspan, 36 feet 5 inches; length, 38 feet 1 inch.
Weight: Empty, 11,095lb; loaded, 23,250lb.

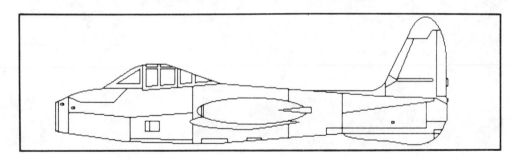

Name: F-94B Starfire.
Manufacturer: Lockheed.
Powerplant: One Allison J33-A-33 turbojet rated at 4600lb thrust and 6000lb thrust with after-
    burning.
Performance: 606 mph at 35,000 feet.
Dimensions: Wingspan, 38 feet 11 inches; length, 40 feet 1 inch.
Weight: Empty, 9557lb; loaded, 12,919lb.

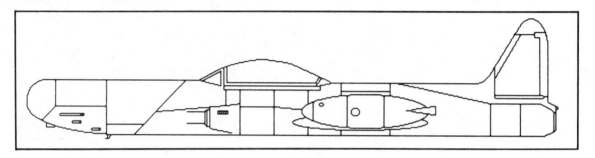

Name: A-4E Skyhawk.
Manufacturer: Douglas.
Powerplant: One Pratt & Whitney J52-P-6A turbojet rated at 8500lb thrust.
Performance: 578 mph at 30,000 feet.
Dimensions: Wingspan, 27 feet 6 inches; length, 42 feet 10.75 inches.
Weight: Empty, 9284lb; loaded, 24,500lb.

Name: F-100D Super Sabre.
Manufacturer: North American.
Powerplant: One Pratt & Whitney J57-P-21A turbojet rated at 11,700lb thrust and 16,950lb thrust with afterburning.
Performance: 864 mph at 35,000 feet.
Dimensions: Wingspan, 38 feet 9 inches; length, 47 feet.
Weight: Empty, 21,000lb; loaded, 34,832lb.

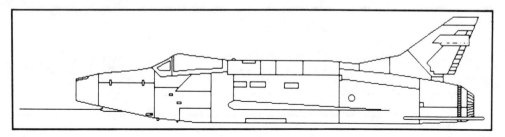

Name: F-105D Thunderchief.
Manufacturer: Republic.
Powerplant: One Pratt & Whitney J75-P-19W turbojet rated at 17,200lb thrust and 24,500lb thrust with afterburning.
Performance: 1122 mph at 50,000 feet.
Dimensions: Wingspan, 34 feet 11.25 inches; length, 67 feet.
Weight: Empty, 28,000lb; loaded, 52,546lb.

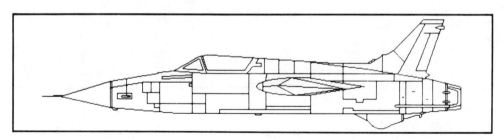

Name: F-4E Phantom II (An RF-4F is illustrated).
Manufacturer: McDonnell.
Powerplant: Two GE J79-GE-17 turbojets each rated at 10,900lb thrust and 17,900lb thrust with afterburning.
Performance: 1450 mph at 36,000 feet.
Dimensions: Wingspan, 38 feet 5 inches; length, 63 feet.
Weight: Empty, 30,073lb; loaded, 57,400lb.

Name: MiG-21 Fishbed.
Manufacturer: Mikoyan-Gurevich.
Powerplant: One Tumansky R-25 turbojet rated at 13,000lb thrust and 19,850lb thrust with after-
   burning.
Performance: 1385 mph at 36,000 feet.
Dimensions: Wingspan, 23 feet 6 inches; length, 51 feet 9 inches.
Weight: Empty, 13,500lb; loaded, 22,000lb.

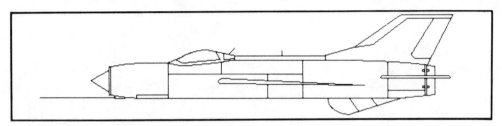

Name: B-52G Stratofortress.
Manufacturer: Boeing.
Powerplant: Eight Pratt & Whitney J57-P-43WB turbojets each rated at 13,750lb thrust.
Performance: 595 mph at 55,000 feet.
Dimensions: Wingspan, 185 feet; length, 160 feet 11 inches.
Weight: Empty, 158,737lb; loaded, 488,000lb.

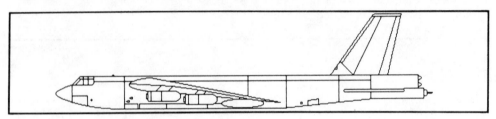

Name: A-7E Corsair II.
Manufacturer: Vought.
Powerplant: One Allison/Rolls-Royce TF41-A-2 turbojet rated at 15,000lb thrust.
Performance: 691 mph at 36,000 feet.
Dimensions: Wingspan, 38 feet 9 inches; length, 46 feet 1.5 inches.
Weight: Empty, 19,111lb; loaded, 42,000lb.

Name: A-6A Intruder.
Manufacturer: Grumman.
Powerplant: Two Pratt & Whitney J52-P-6 turbojets each rated at 8500lb thrust.
Performance: 575 mph at 28,000 feet.
Dimensions: Wingspan, 53 feet; length, 54 feet 7 inches.
Weight: Empty, 25,684lb; loaded 54,000lb.

Name: F-8E Crusader.
Manufacturer: Vought.
Powerplant: One Pratt & Whitney J57-P-20A turbojet rated at 10,700lb thrust and 18,000lb thrust
    with afterburning.
Performance: 1120 mph at 36,000 feet.
Dimensions: Wingspan, 35 feet 2 inches; length, 54 feet 6 inches.
Weight: Empty, 19,925lb; loaded, 34,000lb.

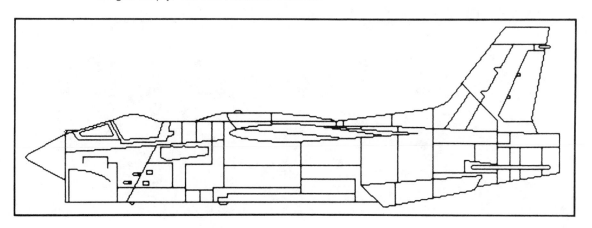

Name: Mirage IIICJ.
Manufacturer: Dassault-Breguet.
Powerplant: One SNECMA Atar O9C turbojet rated at 9436lb thrust and 13,625lb thrust with afterburning.
Performance: 870 mph at 39,370 feet.
Dimensions: Wingspan, 26 feet 11.5 inches; length, 49 feet 3.7 inches.
Weight: Empty, 15,543lb; loaded, 29,762lb.

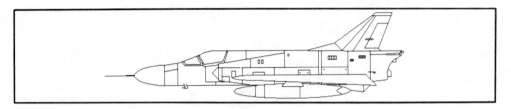

Name: MiG-23.
Manufacturer: Mikoyan-Gurevich.
Powerplant: One Tumansky R-29B turbojet rated at 17,500lb thrust and 25,350lb thrust with afterburning.
Performance: 1550 mph at 40,000 feet.
Dimensions: Wingspan, 46 feet 9 inches; length, 59 feet 10 inches.
Weight: Empty, 25,000lb; loaded, 41,000lb.

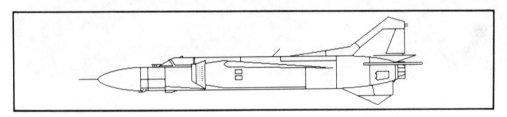

Name: F-111F (An FB-111A is illustrated).
Manufacturer: General Dynamics.
Powerplant: Two Pratt & Whitney TF30-P-100 turbojets each rated at 11,500lb thrust and 25,100 thrust with afterburning.
Performance: 1450 mph at 35,000 feet.
Dimensions: Wingspan, 63 feet; length, 73 feet 6 inches.
Weight: Empty, 47,175lb; loaded, 100,000lb.

Name: Mirage F1.C.
Manufacturer: Dassault-Breguet.
Powerplant: One SNECMA Atar 9K50 turbojet rated at 10,362lb thrust and 15,906lb thrust with afterburning.
Performance: 1442 mph at 40,000 feet.
Dimensions: Wingspan, 27 feet 8.3 inches; length, 50 feet.
Weight: Empty, 16,314lb; loaded, 33,510lb.

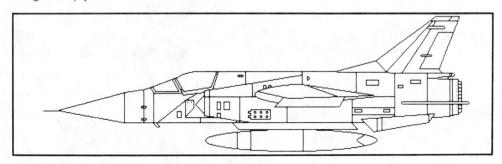

Name: Vulcan B. Mk. 2.
Manufacturer: Hawker Siddeley.
Powerplant: Four Bristol Siddeley Olympus 301 turbojets each rated at 20,000lb thrust.
Performance: 645 mph at 40,000 feet.
Dimensions: Wingspan, 111 feet; length, 99 feet 11 inches.
Weight: Loaded, 200,000lb.

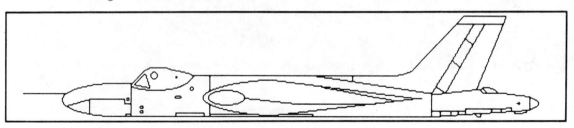

Name: Sea Harrier FRS.1.
Manufacturer: British Aerospace.
Powerplant: One Rolls-Royce Pegasus MK. 104 turbojet rated at 21,500lb thrust.
Performance: 737 mph at 36,000 feet.
Dimensions: Wingspan, 25 feet 3 inches; length, 47 feet 7 inches.
Weight: Empty, 12,960lb; loaded, 26,200lb.

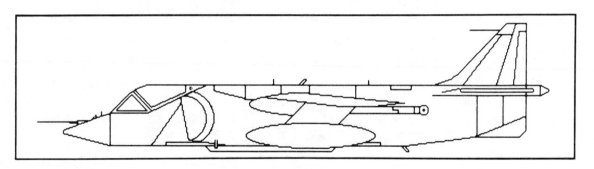

Name: F-14A Tomcat.
Manufacturer: Grumman.
Powerplant: Two Pratt & Whitney TF30-P-412A turbojets each rated at 20,900 with afterburning.
Performance: 1564 mph at 56,000 feet.
Dimensions: Wingspan, 64 feet 1.5 inches; length, 61 feet 2 inches.
Weight: Empty, 39,310lb; loaded, 74,348lb.

Name: MiG-25 Foxbat.
Manufacturer: Mikoyan-Gurevich.
Powerplant: Two Tumansky R-31 turbojets each rated at 20,500lb thrust and 27,120lb thrust with
    afterburning.
Performance: 1870 mph at 78,000 feet.
Dimensions: Wingspan, 46 feet; length, 73 feet 2 inches.
Weight: Empty, 44,000lb; loaded, 82,500lb.

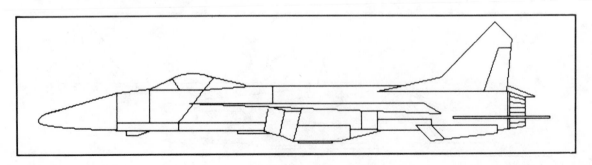

Name: A-10A Thunderbolt II.
Manufacturer: Fairchild.
Powerplant: Two GE TF34-GE-100 turbojets each rated at 9,065lb thrust.
Performance: 439 mph at 5,000 feet.
Dimensions: Wingspan, 57 feet 6 inches; length, 53 feet 4 inches.
Weight: Empty, 24,959lb; loaded, 50,000lb.

Name: MiG-29.
Manufacturer: Mikoyan-Gurevich.
Powerplant: Two Tumansky R-33D turbojets each rated at 11,245lb thrust and 18,300lb thrust
    with afterburning.
Performance: 1452 mph at 52,000 feet.
Dimensions: Wingspan, 33 feet 7.5 inches; length, 50 feet 10 inches.
Weight: Empty, 17,250lb; loaded, 36,275lb.

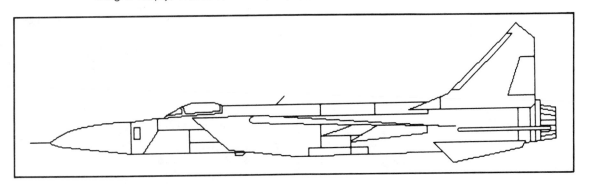

Name: F-15 Eagle.
Manufacturer: McDonnell Douglas.
Powerplant: Two Pratt & Whitney F100-PW-100 turbojets each rated at 23,800lb thrust with after-
    burning.
Performance: 921 mph at 63,000 feet.
Dimensions: Wingspan, 42 feet 10 inches; length, 63 feet 9 inches.
Weight: Empty, 28,000lb; loaded, 56,000lb.

Glossary

AAA—Antiaircraft artillery.

AAM—Air-to-air missile.

ace—a term applied to a pilot who scores a minimum of five aerial kills.

ACM—Air Combat Maneuvering, a U.S. Navy term for dogfighting.

ACT—Air Combat Tactics, a U.S. Air Force term for dogfighting.

ADF—Automatic Direction Finder.

AGL—Above Ground Level, or aircraft altitude above the ground.

AGM—Air-to-ground missile.

air-to-ground—An aerially initiated ground strike.

airfoil—A lift-producing shape.

ailerons—Control surfaces for banks and rolls.

altimeter—An altitude measuring instrument which commonly reads the atmospheric pressure for determining the aircraft's current height.

ARM—Anti-radiation missile.

ATC—Air Traffic Control.

ATIS—Automatic Terminal Information Service.

bail out—*See* punch out.

bandit—A common U.S. pilot term for an enemy aircraft.

bank—A roll maneuver.

bearing—A horizontal direction indication.

bogey—An unidentified approaching aircraft.

bolter—Missing the arresting cable of an aircraft carrier during landing.

break—A high-performance turn.

burner—Slang term for a jet's afterburner.

buster—Slang term for 100 percent engine power exclusive of afterburner.

187

CAG—Carrier Air Group Commander.
CAP—Combat Air Patrol.
ceiling—The altitude of the lowest portion of the present cloud layer.
chord—The width of the wing from its leading edge to its trailing edge.
clock—Location positions relative to the aircraft's orientation that are presented in terms of the numeric values on an analog clock face, e.g., 12 o'clock is straight ahead and 6 o'clock is the airplane's tail.
com—Radio communication.
cruising altitude—An altitude that is maintained during level flight.

deck—The minimal altitude of the current ground over.
density altitude—An adjusted altitude with reference to a fixed standard atmospheric altitude.
dihedral—The upward angle of a lifting surface.
DME—Distance Measuring Equipment.
DOD—Department of Defense.
drag—The frictional force created by the aircraft moving through the air.

ECM—Electronic countermeasures.
elevator—Control surface for upward and downward pitch.
ETA—Estimated time of arrival.
ETD—Estimated time of departure.
ETE—Estimated time enroute.

FAA—Federal Aviation Administration.
FAC—Forward Air Controller.
flak—The aerial bomb burst from an AAA shell.
flaps—A movable surface for increased lift and drag.
fox—A coded radio signal for an air-to-air missile launch.

GCI—Ground-controlled intercept; a ground-based target identification system.
ground speed—The speed of the aircraft relative to the ground.

heading—The compass direction that the aircraft is currently traveling.
HF—High Frequency.
HSI—Horizontal Situation Indicator.
HUD—Head-Up Display.
hypergolic—Compounds that ignite on contact with each other.

IAF—Initial Approach Fix.
IAS—Indicated airspeed.
IFR—Instrument Flight Rules.
ILS—Instrument Landing System.
INS—Inertial Navigation System.
ITT—Inlet turbine temperature.

jinking—A defensive air maneuver, randomly altering an aircraft's heading and altitude.

kill—The destruction of an intended target.
knots—Nautical miles per hour.

LF—Low Frequency.
LOC—Localizer, the horizontal guidance subsystem of the ILS.

Mach—A ratio of true airspeed and the speed of sound; Mach 1 equals 760 mph at sea level.
mayday—An international distress call.

NAS—Naval Air Station.
NATO—North Atlantic Treaty Organization.
nautical mile—*see* nm.
nav—Navigation radio.
navaid—A navigational ground station which transmits VOR or NDB.
NDB—Nondirectional beacon.
NFO—Naval Flight Officer; exclusive of the pilot.
nm—Nautical mile; equals 6076.115 feet or 1852 meters.

OBI—Omni-Bearing Indicator.
OBS—Omni-Bearing Selector.
overshoot—A faster offensive aircraft suddenly moving in front of the target aircraft. This places the offensive aircraft in a defensive posture.

pitch—The upward and downward movement of an aircraft's nose.
pitot-static tube—An external air pressure sensor.
punch out—Emergency ejection from an aircraft.

rate of climb—A feet per minute measurement of the aircraft's current climb rate.
RIO—Radar Intercept Officer; a non-pilot aircrew member. A U.S. Navy term.
RMI—Radio Magnetic Indicator.
RNAV—Area navigation.
ROE—Rules of engagement; predetermined criteria for engaging the enemy.
roll—Horizontal axis rotation.
rotate—The point where the nosewheel leaves the runway during takeoff.
rpm—Revolutions per minute.

SAC—Strategic Air Command.
SAM—Surface-to-air missile.
SID—Standard Instrument Departure.
six—A slang term for the tail position of an aircraft, i.e., 6 o'clock.
skid—A slide out of a turn.
slip—A sideways drop out of a turn.
sortie—A single aerial mission of one aircraft.
STAR—Standard Terminal Arrival Route.

TAS—True airspeed.
TCA—Terminal Control Area.
Top Gun—A U.S. Navy air combat training school at Miramar NAS, California.
touch-and go—A simulated landing approach.
transceiver—A radio that is able to both transmit and receive signals.
transponder—Enhances the aircraft's radar reflection.
trim—Small adjustment surfaces found on the major control surfaces.
true airspeed—An aircraft's real speed through the air with reference to undisturbed air.

turn and bank indicator—Diplays the aircraft's current attitude.

VFR—Visual Flight Rules.
VHF—Very High Frequency.
VLF—Very Low Frequency.
VNAV—Vertical Navigation.
VOR—Very High Frequency Omnidirectional Radio Range.
VSI—Vertical Speed Indicator; also rate of climb indicator.

waypoint—An RNAV generated VOR.
WSO—Weapons System Officer; a non-pilot aircrew member. A U.S. Air Force term.

yaw—Vertical axis rotation.
yoke—The control stick or joystick.
yo-yo—A vertical defensive aerial combat maneuver.

Edited by Steven H. Mesner

Index